THE LITTLE BLUE BOOK OF
NURSES' WISDOM

EDITED BY
NACOLE T. RICCABONI, MSN, APRN
FOREWORD BY PATRICK McMURRAY, BSN, RN

Skyhorse Publishing

Skyhorse Publishing books may be purchased in bulk at special discounts
for sales promotion, corporate gifts, fund-raising, or educational purposes.
Special editions can also be created to specifications. For details, contact the
Special Sales Department, Skyhorse Publishing, 307 West 36th Street, 11th
Floor, New York, NY 10018 or info@skyhorsepublishing.com.

Skyhorse® and Skyhorse Publishing® are registered trademarks of Skyhorse
Publishing, Inc.®, a Delaware corporation.

Visit our website at www.skyhorsepublishing.com.

10 9 8 7 6 5 4 3 2

Library of Congress Cataloging-in-Publication Data is available on file.

Cover design by David Ter-Avanesyan
Edited by Nicole Frail

Print ISBN: 978-1-5107-6741-6
Ebook ISBN: 978-1-5107-6742-3

Printed in China

To my amazing husband and best friend, William.
Thank you for always supporting me. I freaking love you.
To my three incredible, adventurous sons, Rocco, Lucca,
and Nicco. Never stop being curious, continue to love big,
and remain true to yourselves.

Contents

Foreword

by Patrick McMurray, BSN, RN
@PatMacRN

I was first introduced to Nacole Riccaboni via Instagram (@nursenacole), where she shares her voice as one of the handful of nurses with a significant presence on social media. Nacole's willingness to be open about her nursing journey has been invaluable and has helped me navigate my own nursing path as my authentic self.

Arguably, one of the most nuclear facts about the profession of nursing is that it is in a perpetual state of metamorphosis in one way or another. Nursing is simultaneously a complex science and an art. A nursing career brings incredible demands and great rewards, leading to a curiously complex configuration of emotions and challenges. Our work, as nurses, often asks us to show up in intimate ways for communities, even those for which we are not members.

This book acts as a haven for those immersed in the world of nursing. It provides an opportunity for nurses to wrap themselves in words of validation and comfort, and inspiration. Nacole has curated a collection of quotes that encapsulate the incredibly vast array of moments and situations that nurses find themselves confronting daily. This book is a must-have for all nurses. In these pages, you will find words for those soaring moments of humanity and the moments that challenge us to grow and change.

Introduction

Nursing is a unique profession that will fill your heart and, at the same time, empty your tank. You will work countless hours forming community bonds and lasting relationships. You will impact the ones around you with your attention to detail, caregiving, and unwavering advocacy. Your tasks will not be singular, one-dimensional objectives but rather diverse, multifaceted checkboxes that you will work on and implement to improve your patients' health outcomes.

Nursing is a profession that cannot be quantified in one sentence, and nurses aren't individuals who have linear mindsets. Whether you are a nurse, know a nurse, or are on your way to being a nurse, this book will remind you of just how great nursing is and just how much love the nursing profession offers people around the world.

Read and reflect on each quote. Allow these words to touch your heart and trigger memories of your present and future self. Nursing isn't merely a profession; it is a mindset. Let your mood be empowered and encouraged by these wonderful messages.

I.

Learning

Learning is an important part of nursing, and it doesn't end once you graduate from nursing school. Each shift—each patient—is an encounter that you will learn from. Whether you're completing a task on medications or emotional intelligence, you will leave these experiences with a special something.

Everyone raves about how learning is such a positive journey, but it can also be slightly disheartening, in my experience. Regularly coming up short, continually not seeing the full picture, can cause you to second-guess yourself. Those who see these shortcomings—know you are not alone and that we all start there. I started there and you must give yourself time to acclimate to your environment and develop your professional skills.

Many nurses learn on the job, and this may seem daunting, but take it one day at a time. Enter each of your patients' rooms with a full heart and open mind. No one is expecting perfection.

You are a human who is learning to care for people from all walks of life. Each experience will teach you something you didn't know and will expand your mindset regarding a certain disease process or human condition. Your education is a road map that provides great guidance and pathways, but humans don't always function that way. We are unique, with our own presentations and concerns. That can't be taught; it can only be learned through involvement.

Give yourself time to learn from your experiences and let them complement your educational background. You will never stop learning and growing; don't consider this milestone of graduation an end point. It is merely the beginning.

"Any fool can know. The point is to understand."
—ALBERT EINSTEIN

• • •

"Tell me and I forget. Teach me and I remember.
Involve me and I learn."
—BENJAMIN FRANKLIN

• • •

"You don't learn to walk by following rules.
You learn by doing, and by falling over."
—RICHARD BRANSON

• • •

"That which we persist in doing becomes easier for us to do; not that the nature of the thing itself is changed, but that our power to do is increased."
—RALPH WALDO EMERSON

• • •

"Every student can learn, just not on the same day, or the same way."
—GEORGE EVANS

• • •

"The key to pursuing excellence is to embrace an organic, long-term learning process, and not to live in a shell of static, safe mediocrity. Usually, growth comes at the expense of previous comfort or safety."
—JOSH WAITZKIN

• • •

Learning

"Learning is not attained by chance, it must be sought
for with ardor and attended to with diligence."
—Abigail Adams

• • •

"There is no end to education. It is not that you read a book,
pass an examination, and finish with education. The whole of
life, from the moment you are born to the moment you die,
is a process of learning."
—Jiddu Krishnamurti

• • •

"The ultimate lesson all of us have to learn is unconditional love,
which includes not only others but ourselves as well."
—Elisabeth Kubler

• • •

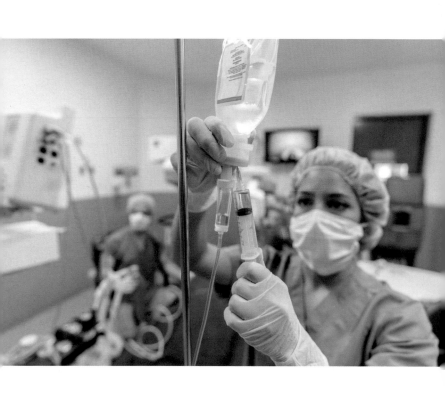

II.

Labor of Love

Nursing is a very labor-intensive profession, from turning, to lifting, to pulling, to pushing patients. Each and every nurse gets a workout when they're working. Whether you're in labor and delivery or orthopedics, you give your whole body to your patients during your shift. Nursing is a team-based endeavor, but there are many moments the solo attribute is present. In those moments, we, as nurses, home in on our caregiving. I've seen nurses focus on their caregiving so much that they skip lunch or even standard self-care practices (which I don't recommend but have been there). And with that in mind, I want this section to remind you that you deserve love, as well. You provide your patients with so much love that there might not be any left when you are alone or with your loved ones. Allow this section to fill your cups and remind you to care for yourself, too. You deserve the same love you give your community and team members day after day. You shouldn't receive the leftover love, the drops of energy remaining. You deserve the same quality you give out: high quality.

When I close my eyes and review my professional career, I see myself running to code blues, getting medications for my patients, and swiftly performing tasks. There seemed to always be a sense of urgency and heightened emphasis in terms of my level of responsibility and time management. Caring for many people simultaneously isn't something that just happens without proper planning and organization. Each year you spend in nursing means having more tools in your toolkit, more skills you have perfected, and more creative ways to solve problems. The labor of love is the profession itself and each nurse's commitment to excellence. From turning to lifting, to cleaning to assisting, a nurse's shift is filled with genuine labor. The labor is in our legs, arms, and minds. We love our communities, and our labor of love shows that dedication. We must calibrate our labor and save some for ourselves, our lives. Take the same professionalism and direct it inward toward the things and people you love.

"Talk to yourself like you would to someone you love."
—Brené Brown

• • •

"There is honor in all work, in all tasks, but take it one step further. Make what you do a labor of love. Then your work will truly touch and change the world in the way you desire. The work you do, whatever your chosen field, will be work that heals."
—Melody Beattie

• • •

"Be patient with yourself. Self-growth is tender; it's holy ground. There's no greater investment."
—Stephen Covey

• • •

"One of the symptoms of an approaching nervous breakdown is the belief that one's work is terribly important."
—Bertrand Russell

• • •

"When you recover or discover something that nourishes
your soul and brings joy, care enough about yourself
to make room for it in your life."
—JEAN SHINODA BOLEN

• • •

"Love yourself enough to set boundaries. Your time and energy
are precious. You get to choose how you use it. You teach people
how to treat you by deciding what you will and won't accept."
—ANNA TAYLOR

• • •

"Hard work is painful when life is devoid of purpose. But when
you live for something greater than yourself and the gratification
of your own ego, then hard work becomes a labor of love."
—STEVE PAVLINA

• • •

Labor of Love

"It's not what you achieve, it's what you overcome.
That's what defines your career."
—CARLTON FISK

• • •

"Just don't give up trying to do what you really want to do. Where
there is love and inspiration, I don't think you can go wrong."
—ELLA FITZGERALD

• • •

"You can only become truly accomplished at something you love.
Don't make money your goal. Instead, pursue the things you
love doing and then do them so well that people can't take their
eyes off of you."
—MAYA ANGELOU

• • •

III.

Caregiving

It takes a certain amount of strength to walk into someone's life at their worst moment and work within that fear and anxiety. To be able to function, maintain your sanity, and remain positive are things each nurse manages with each patient interaction. You process your emotions about being a participant and put all your focus into taking care of your patient and their loved ones. There might be one patient, but we update and notify family members throughout the patient's care. We know our patient's grandchildren, their pets' names, and even their favorite foods. We form relationships, and those bonds allow us to grow as human beings. I've been a patient a few times in the hospital setting, and the nurses were the ones supporting me emotionally in my times of vulnerability. The nurses got me through the tough, stressful times when my family wasn't available. In those moments, I truly understood just how important and meaningful the nurse relationship was.

You might not be the sister, the husband, or the mother, but you are there. You are present, and you are caring for people in their weakest time. There is something to simply being present and witnessing the goings-on of the human body. Each vital sign, each response will be witnessed, measured, and evaluated. The level of detail it takes to manage the critically ill can't be written or understood in text form. Caregiving isn't just a job for nurses, and it isn't something that goes the exact same way each and every time. I've had many experiences that involved the same disease process with varying responses and outcomes. One patient would recover with no complications, while another patient with the same disease process would decompensate. The body can only take so much, and each person has different starting points and impact capability. Healthcare is fickle. The unpredictability of caregiving has its own stress factor, and nurses will walk into that uncertainty with poise. Take this section as a reminder of all the quantifiable and nonquantifiable attributes nurses bring to their communities on a given day.

"Every person in this life has something to teach me—and as
soon as I accept that, I open myself to truly listening."
—CATHERINE DOUCETTE

• • •

"The most important thing in communication is hearing
what isn't said."
—PETER DRUCKER

• • •

"Kindness can transform someone's dark moment with a blaze of
light. You'll never know how much your caring matters."
—AMY LEIGH MERCREE

• • •

"They may forget what you said,
but they will never forget how you made them feel."
—CARL W. BUEHNER

• • •

"Be in the moment with them. They may not remember
you are there, but YOU do."
—JOYCE O. C.

• • •

"The closest thing to being cared for is to care for someone else."
—CARSON MCCULLERS

• • •

Caregiving

"Caregiving often calls us to lean into love we didn't know possible."
—TIA WALKER

• • •

"There are only four kinds of people in the world: those who have been caregivers, those who are currently caregivers, those who will be caregivers, and those who will need a caregiver."
—ROSALYNN CARTER

• • •

"The disease might hide the person underneath, but there's still a person in there who needs your love and attention."
—Jamie Calandriello

• • •

"When you are a caregiver, you know that every day you will touch a life, or a life will touch yours."
—Unknown

• • •

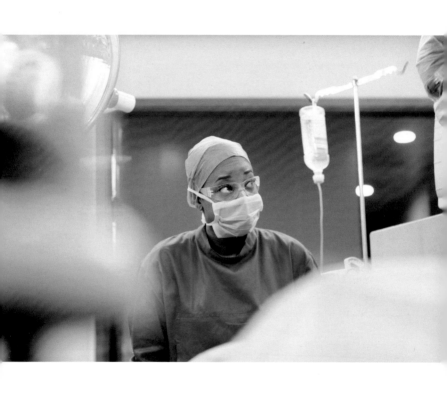

IV.

Dedication

Dedication to a community's well-being is a goal of each caregiver. Nurses complete tasks and follow guidelines in an effort to provide the best healthcare to every individual within their community. Nurses smile when we see someone recover and heal before our eyes. Nurses are deeply saddened when someone deteriorates or has an adverse event. Nurses are dedicated to nursing and the act of providing quality care. Nurses' professionalism remains unwavering and their mindsets are methodical. Nurses take the nursing profession to heart and respect the level of trust the community provides them. Nurses return that trust and respect by providing the highest levels of care and thoughtfulness. Regardless of how their day went or will go, nurses should know that their community appreciates their efforts and continued dedication. Regardless of what is going on, nurses work to give their patients the care they deserve. Whether it is assisting in advocating or reaching out to other medical professionals for assistance, nurses will work on an issue for hours to ensure their patients have their best chances at great outcomes.

Dedication is something that each nurse lives with. It's easy to be dedicated when the outcomes are positive, when everyone is all smiles and laughter. When I picture these moments, I picture an uncomplicated birthing experience. The mother is glowing, and the baby is healthy. But no one discusses dedication in terms of challenging outcomes. Nurses see the good and the bad and both are engrossing. I, myself, was involved in a car accident as a child. It was a nurse who sparked my passion and dedication to the profession. The nurse was dedicated to helping young children who were injured. She understood her role and accepted that she could be a witness to undesirable results. She thrived on knowing she was making an impact, regardless of the outcome being positive or negative. That right there is dedication. Understanding the uncertainty of an outcome and still caring and being devoted to the process. She is every nurse across the world—clocking in, activating their greatness, ready to change the lives of people in their community.

Dedication

"Dedicate yourself to what gives your life true meaning and
purpose; make a positive difference in someone's life."
—ROY T. BENNETT

• • •

"Though you can love what you do not master, you cannot
master what you do not love."
—MOKOKOMA MOKHONOANA

• • •

"When it comes to fighting for your dreams, be a dragon.
Breathe fire."
—RICHELLE E. GOODRICH

• • •

"When you love your work, you will be exceptionally
diligent in what you do, and you will excel in delivering
both quality and quantity."
—DR PREM JAGYASI

• • •

"We overestimate the event and underestimate the process. Every fulfilled dream occurred because of dedication."
—JOHN C. MAXWELL

• • •

"We all have dreams. But in order to make dreams come into reality, it takes an awful lot of determination, dedication, self-discipline, and effort."
—JESSE OWENS

• • •

"There is never just one thing that leads to success for anyone. I feel it's always a combination of passion, dedication, hard work, and being in the right place at the right time."
—LAUREN CONRAD

• • •

Dedication

"Success is not a genetic or inherited factor. Success is a state of mind developed through understanding that risk, perseverance, dedication, and the 'never quit' attitude are the key elements in combination that lead to masterful achievement."

—Byron Pulsifer

• • •

"You never change your life until you step out of your comfort zone; change begins at the end of your comfort zone."

—Roy T. Bennett

• • •

"If we have a goal and a plan, and are willing to take risks and mistakes and work as a team, we can choose to do the hard thing."

—Scott Kelly

• • •

V.

Coping

Nurses want to help and save people. But sadly, the human body can only compensate for so long. As a graduate nurse, I had a thought that everyone could be saved under the right circumstances. As time went on and I gained more and more professional experience, I concluded that view was inaccurate. Regardless of lifestyle or choices, the body is made up of tissues and bones. There will be moments in your nursing career where you perform every intervention available, and it will still end badly. The body can only go so far, and it can only recover so much after certain milestones have occurred. It's unfortunate, but nurses must understand this concept and process these feelings. It's okay to get upset, but it's not okay to blame yourself. Healthcare is emotional; coping with these emotions is a priority. Whether you choose meditation, therapy, crying, or other means, processing these big feelings is essential. Processing and acknowledgement will keep you emotionally healthy.

We hear about how strong nurses are, and this is true, but we must in the same breath discuss proper coping and the need for proper expression. Strong people discuss their concerns and fears. Nurses are not robots; we feel and we must heal from our experiences. Each experience will rub off on you in some shape or form. There will be a metaphorical residue that you must manage. The effects of what nurses see can't be articulated into words, in my opinion. Nurses see too much, we experience too much. Nurses are there, at the bedside, up close and personal. Even if they don't know the individual, they are in the experience and are not merely observers. They are an active participant and said participation and closeness must be parceled and regarded. Each nurse will cope differently, as they process their feelings with different tactics. The goal is to process the feelings, what those feelings invoke, and how they will influence your actions.

"We hardly ever talk about trauma afterwards, because it helps to live in a world where we can pretend it never happened."
—Joyce Rachelle

• • •

"Don't be so hard on yourself. Don't be so hard on loved ones. At the end of the day, we're all just trying to do the best we can."
—Charles F. Glassman

• • •

"If you can't fix what's wrong, you focus on what you can make right."
—Brigid Kemmere

• • •

"You have changed but that is okay. Life is not static,
why should you be?"
—SAMANTHA TAMBURELLO

• • •

"I'm still coping with my trauma, but coping by trying to find
different ways to heal it rather than hide it."
—CLEMANTINE WAMARIYA

• • •

"Resilience isn't a single skill. It's a variety of skills and coping
mechanisms. To bounce back from bumps in the road as well as
failures, you should focus on emphasizing the positive."
—JEAN CHATZKY

• • •

Coping

"We can easily manage if we will only take, each day, the burden appointed to it. But the load will be too heavy for us if we carry yesterday's burden over again today, and then add the burden of the morrow before we are required to bear it."
—JOHN NEWTON

• • •

"We have two strategies for coping; the way of avoidance or the way of attention."
—MARILYN FERGUSON

• • •

"Facing it, always facing it, that's the way to get through. Face it."
—JOSEPH CONRAD

• • •

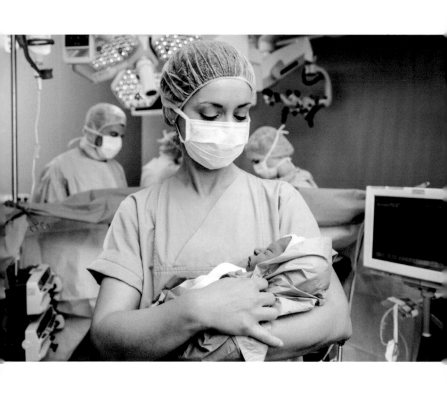

VI.

❧

Motivation

There will be moments in your professional career when you don't think you can go any farther, when you are burned out and exhausted. And guess what? We all have been there, and you are allowed to have those moments. You are a human, taking care of humans who need help. Sometimes, your tank will be running on low or your glass will be almost empty. And still, you will be expected to work a twelve-hour shift. Offices and hospitals have no precise "off hours." People will continue to need healthcare and support, which means you will always be in demand. When you have those moments, I want to you remember your "why"—the reason that motivated you to be become a nurse. That guiding moment that you finally said to yourself: I'm going to do this. Each of us has a story in terms of what brought us into this wonderful profession. Was it because your mother was a nurse and you saw just how much she loved going to work? Or was it an interaction with a nurse in your community? We all have our own why, so what was yours? Write it down.

Motivation is the willingness to do something. What motivates one person might not motivate another. The key here isn't the motivation; it's the action behind the motivation in times of stress. If your motivation is to help people, this will drive you during your most exhausting times. Nurses don't lose their motivation to help people when their feet hurt. They don't just stop caring. They move forward and do what is needed. You must find what motivates you, what calls you in times of anxiety and pain. It will be your reminder, your sign, your flashlight in the dark. It will allow you to see through the fog and chaos, allow you to understand how impactful your actions are. Your motivation will always center your thoughts and ground you to your passage and true calling. *Why* is a funny word. When prompted, it brings up volumes of memories and emotions. Don't be afraid to allow your mind to wander and explore your feelings regarding the nursing profession. There is no good or bad reason, only the truth, and that's enough.

"Success is walking from failure to failure with no loss of enthusiasm."
—WINSTON CHURCHILL

• • •

"The ones who are crazy enough to think they can change
the world are the ones who do."
—ANONYMOUS

• • •

"There are two types of people who will tell you that you cannot
make a difference in this world: those who are afraid to try and
those who are afraid you will succeed."
—RAY GOFORTH

• • •

"Courage is resistance to fear, mastery of fear—
not absence of fear."
—MARK TWAIN

• • •

"When I dare to be powerful, to use my strength in
the service of my vision, then it becomes less and less
important whether I am afraid."
—AUDRE LORDE

• • •

"When something is important enough, you do it even
if the odds are not in your favor."
—ELON MUSK

• • •

"Decide what you want, decide what you are willing to exchange
for it. Establish your priorities and go to work."
—H. L. Hunt

• • •

"Where there is a will, there is a way. If there is a chance in a
million that you can do something, anything, to keep what
you want from ending, do it. Pry the door open or, if need be,
wedge your foot in that door and keep it open."
—Pauline Kael

• • •

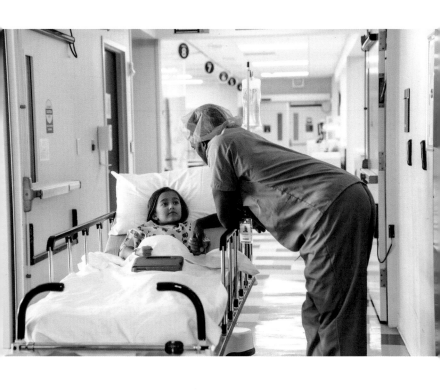

"Consult not your fears but your hopes and your dreams.
Think not about your frustrations, but about your unfulfilled
potential. Concern yourself not with what you tried and failed in,
but with what it is still possible for you to do."
—POPE JOHN XXIII

• • •

"I learned that we can do anything, but we can't do everything . . .
at least not at the same time. So think of your priorities not
in terms of what activities you do, but when you do them.
Timing is everything."
—DAN MILLMAN

• • •

VII.
ᘒ☙

Balance

Work-life balance is essential in the nursing profession. Nurses give all their physical and mental capabilities to each of their patients. Sometimes, they leave work with nothing left for themselves or loved ones. Being dedicated and committed to your community is a noble deed, but do not ignore your own needs and your own priorities. You want to be a nurse, or you are a nurse, but that is not your only identity. You were a person before this profession, with your own personal pathway and objectives. Those needs should not be dismissed or ignored simply because you found a profession you love. Nursing should complement your life and improve your environment with quality and depth. It shouldn't be an anchor or weight you carry around. When you reflect back on your job, do you smile? Do you have special moments with patients or team members? That right there is the icing. But it isn't the cake. The cake is your life outside of work.

Who you are, your support system, your loved ones. They are the layers.

When you go home, your heart should be filled with memories of your day, your hard work, and all the details in between. When you reflect on your profession, it should make you smile, you should be proud. But you should always have a life outside of this setting. Yes, you are nurse, but that isn't your only title. Nurses are fathers, mothers, sons, daughters, cousins, and friends. We had an entire life story before nursing entered our lives. We must respect that personal component and understand it is just as important. Take that vacation, attend your daughter's recital. Those are moments you will not get back. Nursing is a team effort, and when you are home, you must be present (in all aspects). Don't carry a burden home and allow it to eat away at your relationships. You deserve to be happy and to live. Allow for balance. Your family deserves the same compassion you give your patients. No one wants leftovers. Don't treat yourself or your support system to leftover-you. With proper balance, there will be true-you left to give and enjoy your life with.

"Balance is not better time management, but better
boundary management. Balance means making choices
and enjoying those choices."
—BETSY JACOBSON

• • •

"You will never find time for anything.
If you want time, you must make it."
—CHARLES BUXTON

• • •

"We think, mistakenly, that success is the result of the amount of
time we put in at work, instead of the quality of time we put in."
—ARIANNA HUFFINGTON

• • •

"Never get so busy making a living that you forget to make a life."
—DOLLY PARTON

• • •

"You can have it all. You just can't have it all at once."
—OPRAH WINFREY

• • •

"Happiness is not a matter of intensity but of balance
and order and rhythm and harmony."
—THOMAS MERTON

• • •

"Problems arise in that one has to find a balance between what
people need from you and what you need for yourself."
—JESSYE NORM

• • •

"We need to introduce a little balance into your life. Part of this
balance means not missing out on some of the marvels of life
around you, the fun, some excitement, or other challenges in life."
—CATHERINE PULSIFER

• • •

"Balance is key; without balance there's conflict,
a battle between positivity and negativity."
—BRIAN BENJAMIN SOTOMAYOR

• • •

"Balance is not something you find, it's something you create."
—JANA KINGSFORD

• • •

VIII.

Possibilities

Allow yourself the opportunity to discover what you love about nursing. Don't assume you already know, don't allow yourself to build up walls in your mind. Life is unpredictable and evolving. Every time I thought I had my professional path planned out and established, a plot twist would come and change my entire outlook. My interest in nursing changed weekly in nursing school. You can't control what aspect of nursing inspires you, but you can control discovery and embrace possibility. Your nursing journey will have obstacles and unknowns. Allow yourself the ability to find your true passion. Allow yourself to be present and invest in what you want to do in life, not what you should do. There are many nursing opportunities; don't settle because others think it's a "smart" move.

Nursing is a profession with many tracks and routes. From nursing informatics, to nurse practitioner, to community nursing, there are many routes that will feed varying aspects of a nurse's personality. If you love technology, there is something for you. If you love home health, there is an option for you. Whether you choose to work inpatient or outpatient in your community, nursing possibilities are boundless. There are so many varying ways to help individuals within your community. Where you are now might feed your soul in this moment in time. But in the future, your interest might be sparked by another specialty. It's okay to not want to remain stagnant, to have different curiosities. We all grow, and our interests change. Do you have the same interests you had when you were in middle school? I doubt it. We are ever-changing creatures. Sometimes we grow out of a position or profession; it happens. That doesn't mean anything other than that. Being stagnant isn't an accomplishment. Being fearful isn't healthy. Allow yourself the opportunity to want more and go with it.

"Without leaps of imagination or dreaming, we lose the excitement
of possibilities. Dreaming, after all, is a form of planning."
—Gloria Steinem

• • •

"Turn your obstacles into opportunities
and your problems into possibilities."
—Roy T. Bennett

• • •

"Dreams are what guide us, art is what defines us, math is what makes it all possible, and love is what lights our way."
—MIKE NORTON

• • •

"There is a thin line between the impossible and the possible: that is determination."
—OGWO DAVID EMENIKE

• • •

"You can't see it now, but that thing you didn't get will someday be the best thing you never had. Let it go. Better is coming."
—MANDY HALE

• • •

"Remember that things are not always as they appear to be. . . .
Curiosity creates possibilities and opportunities."
—Roy T. Bennett

• • •

"Start by doing what is necessary, then what is possible,
and suddenly you are doing the impossible."
—St. Francis of Assisi

• • •

"Whatsoever you have done is nothing in comparison to that
which you can do. And nothing is whatsoever you can do in
comparison with that which you are."
—Yoda

• • •

"Even if you are not looking at things the wrong way, simply looking at things a different way can bring new possibilities to your attention."
—David A. Hunter

• • •

"Nothing is impossible when you apply the thoughts necessary that support your positive mindset."
—Scott Allan

• • •

"Dwell in possibility."
—Emily Dickinson

• • •

IX.

Difficulties

Every job has its difficult moments. Whether internal or external, each job has certain obstacles that must be dealt with. As a nurse, you will enter the lives of people in your community and see them at their most vulnerable, their weakest. You will wake up, get dressed for work, and be thrown into relationship dynamics and the human condition. It's an unusual bond and yet, every nurse does it over and over again, shift after shift. As nurses, our goal isn't to interpret and judge; we simply examine the situation given and adapt accordingly. Difficulties require adaption, and in times of stress, this process can be overwhelming. Reaching out for help doesn't make you a weak person, nor does it mean you lack knowledge. The human condition can only take so much strain, so when you don't have answers, seek help elsewhere.

Although this sounds negative, difficult times are merely moments in time. They will exist, and as time passes, you and said circumstances will change. No one said nursing was easy, and no one loves the hardships their profession exposes them to. You can dislike an aspect of your profession and still love doing it. Be honest with yourself and allow yourself time to process your feelings of inadequacy and exhaustion. You are a human taking care of sick humans. Your community and team members lean on you a great deal. You need time to process these commitments and the baggage attached. We all have been there and understanding your feelings will allow you the space to process them appropriately. You are not "stronger" if you avoid your feelings related to caregiving. Any unprocessed emotions will resurface in the future and will impact your life and relationships at some point.

"We must accept finite disappointment, but we must never lose infinite hope."
—MARTIN LUTHER KING, JR.

• • •

"The greater the difficulty, the more glory in surmounting it. Skillful pilots gain their reputation from storms and tempests."
—EPICTETUS

• • •

"Courage doesn't always roar. Sometimes courage is the quiet voice at the end of the day, saying, 'I will try again tomorrow.'"
—MARY ANNE RADMACHER

• • •

"Resilience isn't a single skill. It's a variety of skills and coping mechanisms. To bounce back from bumps in the road as well as failures, you should focus on emphasizing the positive."
—JEAN CHATZKY

• • •

"When we learn how to become resilient, we learn how to embrace the beautifully broad spectrum of the human experience."
—JAEDA DEWALT

• • •

"The greatest glory in living lies not in never failing, but in rising every time we fail."
—NELSON MANDELA

• • •

"In times of great stress or adversity, it's always best to keep busy, to plow your anger and your energy into something positive."
—Lee Iacocca

• • •

"We must embrace pain and burn it as fuel for our journey."
—Kenji Miyazawa

• • •

"The best way to get rid of the pain is to feel the pain. And when you feel the pain and go beyond it, you'll see there's a very intense love that is wanting to awaken itself."
—Deepak Chopra

• • •

"To succeed, you have to do something and be very bad at it for a while. You have to look bad before you can look really good."
—Barbara DeAngelis

• • •

X.

Connection

Connection is what life is about. Listening, understanding, and support is what everyone strives toward. We aren't as different as we think. We all want and encourage bonding with the people who provide light and substance in our lives. As a nurse, I never considered the importance of this concept until I graduated from nursing school. The hospital isn't a place of positivity (usually). It's where the sick reside, where the ill recover. Loneliness and stress can occur in some patients. And as nurses, we see individuals who are in emotional distress regarding their condition or the future. An admission for treatment can be life changing or life ending—the severity varies. Nurses appreciate these varying levels of readiness and meet them head on with compassion and support. Nurses see these monumental moments and respect their importance through work and empathy. Nurses walk into these situations with positivity and strength each and every time they clock in.

Nurses don't fear tough conversations, and they don't shy away from reality. Nurses know just how delicate the human condition is and work toward providing the proper support system so many people deserve and need. From my husband's heart attack to my complicated cesarean section, nurses were there and got us through those tough times. Nurses have no idea how much they matter and how many lives they touch on a daily basis. I'd never be able to quantify how much I needed the nurses as a patient. The connection was my lifeline, and I still appreciate their efforts to this day. As a patient, I remember being vulnerable, both emotionally and physically, and nurses were there and cared for both parts. Whether I was crying because I missed my children or crying because I was in pain, nurses were there and willing to assist me. When my husband was in the hospital post-surgery, nurses were the ones to educate us both on what to expect and how to prepare him for discharge. It was and will always be nurses who connect with their community in this way. This way that hugs them and says, "You can do this and here is what you need to know."

"I define connection as the energy that exists between people when they feel seen, heard, and valued; when they can give and receive without judgment; and when they derive sustenance and strength from the relationship."
—Brené Brown

• • •

"Sometimes, reaching out and taking someone's hand is the beginning of a journey. At other times, it is allowing another to take yours."
—Vera Nazarian

• • •

"Think back to the most important experiences of your life, the highest highs, the greatest victories, the most daunting obstacles overcome. How many happened to you alone? I bet there are very few. When you understand that being connected to others is one of life's greatest joys, you realize that life's best comes when you initiate and invest in solid relationships."
—JOHN C. MAXWELL

• • •

"Healing yourself is connected with healing others."
—YOKO ONO

• • •

"Listening is an attitude of the heart, a genuine desire to be with another which both attracts and heals."
—SURA HART

• • •

"Deep human connection is . . . the purpose and the result of a meaningful life—and it will inspire the most amazing acts of love, generosity, and humanity."
—MELINDA GATES

• • •

"The business of business is relationships; the business of life is human connection."
—ROBIN SHARMA

• • •

"People find meaning and redemption in the most
unusual human connections."
—Khaled Hosseini

• • •

"You have to make a space in your heart, in your mind,
and in your life itself for authentic human connection."
—Marianne Williamson

• • •

"Human connections are deeply nurtured in
the field of shared story."
—Jean Houston

• • •

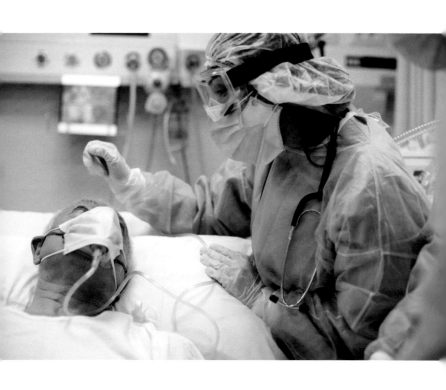

XI.

Honesty

Honesty is harder than most people think. Everyone says they are honest when the information presented has no weight to it. When compliments and positive messages are given, honesty flows out of us with ease. No hesitation, no contemplation regarding the ramifications of the words that are verbalized. But nursing occurs in times of sadness as well as happiness, and honesty in those times can be challenging. Healthcare is not just medicine; it's emotional and requires a certain level of tenderness and caring. We all want the best outcomes for our patients, but sadly, that doesn't always happen. Often, I'm making the late-night call to a spouse or parent about their loved one deteriorating. These moments tear me up, because no one is ever prepared, nor should they be. Being woken up has its own level of emotional unreadiness, without the news being a part of it. Pile on the worst news being given, and it's simply an overwhelming experience with many layers of strain.

You are the person, the only person, delivering news that will change their entire life. And yet, nurses boldly walk into those conversations with kindness and honesty. Nurses understand the fragility of the setting and respect the importance of this moment. They don't simply deliver medications and perform tasks; nurses shape relationships and life journeys of those within their communities. Honesty regarding the situation, circumstances, and overall kindness is what separates nurses from other professionals. It isn't the phrasing or disposition that shapes honesty; it is warmth and honor. Nurses honor themselves and their communities through their performance. Even when honesty hurts or will hurt, it's required and it's nurses who accept what must be done and respect their patients enough to proceed with the most professional and warmest way possible.

"Goodness is about character—integrity, honesty, kindness, generosity, moral courage, and the like. More than anything else, it is about how we treat other people."
—Dennis Prager

• • •

"Honesty is grounded in humility and indeed in humiliation, and in admitting exactly where we are powerless."
—David Whyte

• • •

"The most important factors for any artist are the honesty towards one's craft, hard work, and passion that guides them."
—Anupriya Goenka

• • •

"If you wanted to do something absolutely honest, something true, it always turned out to be a thing that had to be done alone."
—RICHARD YATES

• • •

"The simple step of a courageous individual is not to take part in the lie. One word of truth outweighs the world."
—ALEKSANDR I. SOLZHENITSYN

• • •

"The real things haven't changed. It is still best to be honest and truthful; to make the most of what we have; to be happy with simple pleasures; and have courage when things go wrong."
—LAURA INGALLS WILDER

• • •

"To share your weakness is to make yourself vulnerable;
to make yourself vulnerable is to show your strength."
—CRISS JAMI

• • •

"Seeking what is true is not seeking what is desirable."
—ALBERT CAMUS

• • •

"Better to get hurt by the truth than comforted with a lie."
—KHALED HOSSEINI

• • •

"Integrity is telling myself the truth. And honesty is
telling the truth to other people."
—SPENCER JOHNSON

• • •

XII.

Leadership

Nursing, like all careers, has levels, and one level is leadership. As you work in the field of nursing, there are opportunities in leadership that might present themselves. I never understood the importance of leadership until I was in the position myself. It's one thing to manage the care of a group of patients, but it's another thing to manage an entire floor, as well as supporting the nurses who care for said individuals. That level of responsibility is immense and can pull an individual in different directions. In terms of nursing leadership, there are education, management, and policymaking pathways. Each pathway has its own objectives and concerns regarding the delivery of medical care. Each person brings their own perspectives and skills to the table, and with that comes a multitude of past experiences and guidance. No leader is the same, no policy is alike. Each nurse brings years of experience and knowledge to the table.

Nurses must use their team members (and themselves) to advance the nursing profession and allow for positive constructive change within the field. No one understands nursing like a nurse— that can't be disputed. There are no substitutions. Understand that what you do and how you think can be the keys to unlocking the future of nursing and its advancement. Leadership isn't about academia, nor is it about title; it's about awareness, disruption, and impact. All these things can be done by you—when you decide it is time—when you see a need and are ready for change. Disruption seems unsettling, but true change can only occur with someone being brave enough to evaluate the status-quo and determine something better is possible. Who else would elevate the field of nursing than individuals within the profession who experience the culture on a daily basis, who see the gaps and needs within their community?

"Every time you open your mouth,
it's an opportunity for leadership."
—BENJAMIN ZANDER

• • •

"You don't build a house without its foundation.
You don't build a hospital without its nurses."
—ANONYMOUS

• • •

"Where the needs of the world and your talents cross,
there lies your vocation."
—ARISTOTLE

• • •

"To accomplish great things, you must not only act but also dream, not only plan but also believe."
—ANATOLE FRANCE

• • •

"Nurses will play a fundamental role in shaping the new paradigm of healthcare."
— OLYMPIA SNOWE

• • •

"Leadership is developing things in parallel and knowing when they will converge."
—Robert Ballard

• • •

Leadership

"Effective leadership is putting first things first. Effective management is discipline, carrying it out."
—STEPHEN COVEY

• • •

"Lead and inspire people. Don't try to manage and manipulate people. Inventories can be managed but people must be led."
—ROSS PEROT

• • •

"Leadership is unlocking people's potential to become better."

—BILL BRADLEY

• • •

"One of the tests of leadership is the ability to recognize a problem before it becomes an emergency."
—ARNOLD GLASOW

• • •

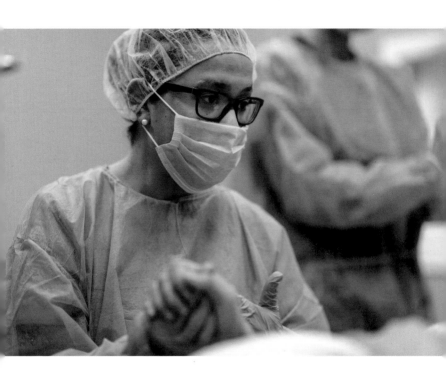

XIII.

Strength

As a graduate nurse, I felt so unprepared and scrawny. I was about to enter a profession filled with strong, capable individuals who walked into stressful situations voluntarily. Don't get me wrong, I understood what nursing involved, but I never considered myself to be strong. I had never been in serious situations and never had to allocate my feelings while taking care of someone who was dying. It wasn't until my first shift that I truly understood the importance of my job and the associated strength that came with it. The dedication, responsibility, and strength required of nurses each shift is immeasurable. Regardless of the level of care, nursing is a force. A force that uplifts a community and provides support and potential. Strength isn't solely about the physical tasks nurses do (because trust me, there are many). It's also about all the emotionally charged, hectic, volatile times that make the job more than a job.

Strength isn't a single action or time frame. Strength is waking up and making a choice to help your community. Helping with sore feet and aching backs. Nurses enter unpredictable situations and circumstances with still hands and capable minds. On a nurse's worst day, he or she remains mighty. Strength isn't shining in perfection; strength is being present and understanding the process. The process of nursing has many levels with moving parts. No one person is responsible, no one individual is to blame. It's a team effort, with strength residing in the numbers. When you are weak, your team members support you. When you are strong, you seek out weak spots and fortify them. Nurses are stronger together; they work as one and cherish the hard work each person brings to the table. Strength isn't doing something once; it's entering chaos over and over and making a difference. It's being a nurse.

"Strength does not come from physical capacity.
It comes from an indomitable will."
—MAHATMA GANDHI

• • •

"Character cannot be developed in ease and quiet. Only through
experience of trial and suffering can the soul be strengthened,
ambition inspired, and success achieved."
—HELEN KELLER

• • •

"You never know how strong you are
until being strong is your only choice."
—BOB MARLEY

• • •

"You gain strength, courage, and confidence by every experience in which you really stop to look fear in the face. You are able to say to yourself, 'I lived through this horror. I can take the next thing that comes along.'"
—ELEANOR ROOSEVELT

• • •

"Unity is strength . . . when there is teamwork and collaboration, wonderful things can be achieved."
—MATTIE STEPANEK

• • •

"Strength does not come from winning. Your struggles develop your strengths. When you go through hardships and decide not to surrender, that is strength."
—ARNOLD SCHWARZENEGGER

• • •

"I think a hero is an ordinary individual who finds strength to persevere and endure in spite of overwhelming obstacles."
—CHRISTOPHER REEVE

• • •

"You have power over your mind—not outside events. Realize this, and you will find strength."
—MARCUS AURELIUS

• • •

"Fortitude is the marshal of thought, the armor of the will, and the fort of reason."
—FRANCIS BACON

• • •

XIV.

Emotions

Someone once told me that emotions must be placed aside when you clock in, and I disagree with this statement (on certain levels). Yes, it isn't in our best interest to bring our personal problems to work. But no one can fully ignore their feelings when nursing provokes nothing but emotions. Emotions are what drive us to care emotionally and physically for the people in our community. These experiences bury themselves in our psyche and some events change us. People downplay emotions, but they are very powerful and must be respected. Emotions can be buried and ignored, but over time, they will spread into other facets of your life if not processed in a healthy manner. When you take care of people, you will have an emotional response to the experience. Whether you are a nurse assisting in the birthing experience of new mothers, or a palliative care nurse witnessing and assisting with hospice care, your emotions will be involved. Nurses don't simply perform tasks; we experience monumental life moments with the individuals in our community. We are a part of their life stories and the transition within their lives.

Processing emotions is something you do when you are at home and off work. Whether you decided to get therapy or meditate, emotions must be processed and managed. In my opinion, you can't watch someone die without it affecting your emotional state. You don't watch someone experience a bad outcome and simply shrug your shoulders and go to lunch. Yes, in the moment, you are expected to move on, in a way. But once you are in your safe space, you have to allocate the experience and parcel what you have just witnessed. How do you feel about what you did and saw? Do you have any emotions that you don't understand or that you want to speak to someone about? The phrase *emotional well-being* has become a buzzword, but most people swallow their feelings without processing them. Nurses need to take the time to decompress and process their work experiences. The longevity of a nursing career isn't simply based on how well you care for your back and joints; it's also dependent on how well you care for your emotional needs. Like your back, emotions can only tolerate so much weight.

"I think emotional health is a big contributor to physical health."
—April Rose

• • •

"When our emotional health is in a bad state, so is our level of self-esteem. We have to slow down and deal with what is troubling us, so that we can enjoy the simple joy of being happy and at peace with ourselves."
—Jess C. Scott

• • •

"No one cares how much you know,
until they know how much you care."
—Theodore Roosevelt

• • •

"Emotions can get in the way or get you on the way."
—Mavis Mazhura

• • •

"Our feelings are not there to be cast out or conquered.
They're there to be engaged and expressed with
imagination and intelligence."
—T.K. COLEMAN

• • •

"Emotional intelligence is the ability to sense, understand, and
effectively apply the power and acumen of emotions as a source
of human energy, information, connection, and influence."
—ROBERT K. COOPER

• • •

"Your intellect may be confused,
but your emotions will never lie to you."
—ROGER EBERT

• • •

"Anything that's human is mentionable, and anything that is mentionable can be more manageable. When we can talk about our feelings, they become less overwhelming, less upsetting, and less scary."
—FRED ROGERS

• • •

"You don't have to be positive all the time. It's perfectly okay to feel sad, angry, annoyed, frustrated, scared, and anxious. Having feelings doesn't make you a negative person. It makes you human."
—LORI DESCHENE

"Increasing the strength of our minds is the only way to reduce the difficulty of life."
—MOKOKOMA MOKHONOANA

• • •

XV.

꒰•

Shame

One emotion I thought I would never experience in my nursing career is regret. Nursing is a highlight reel of accomplishments and achievements. But hidden in between can be moments of regret or shame. We all try to be our best selves in times of crisis, but we are also human beings balancing and juggling many things at once, from physical demands to emotional stressors. We can only go so far and only do so much with the time and skills given. There will be moments you reflect back and wish you had done something else, acted in a different manner, bitten your tongue, or spoken up regarding a comment. I remember there was a code blue (when I was a fresh graduate nurse), and when I walked into the room, I froze. All the knowledge left my body, and the emotions of the situation got the best of me. I wasn't helpful, I was in the way, I was unproductive.

It wasn't like the textbook, and this person in front of me wasn't a mannequin. He was a real person, with loved ones (crying in the corner), and it all just got real for me. Luckily, my preceptor snapped me out of it, and I did what was needed seconds later. Now, although my freeze was minor seconds, your episode might be longer. You might linger in that haze for minutes to hours. Being in that moment, no matter the time, is okay. You are not perfect, and that expectation isn't fair. Treat yourself with the support and positivity you treat others with. Understand we are all learning and growing, and allow yourself the space needed for those things. No one starts a new job or a new position or enters a new environment knowing what to expect. There will be curve balls. Enter with an open mind and a full heart, knowing that you are on a path of learning, and that might mean you pause or hesitate when you should act, or you act when you should have paused.

"If we can share our story with someone who responds with empathy and understanding, shame can't survive."
—Brené Brown

• • •

"Shame is a soul-eating emotion."
—Carl Gustav Jung

• • •

"Heaven knows we need never be ashamed of our tears, for they are rain upon the blinding dust of earth, overlying our hard hearts."
—Charles Dickens

• • •

"Always do your best. Your best is going to change from moment to moment; it will be different when you are healthy as opposed to sick. Under any circumstance, simply do your best, and you will avoid self-judgment, self-abuse and regret."
—DON MIGUEL RUIZ

• • •

"Regret doesn't remind us that we did badly.
It reminds us that we know we can do better."
—KATHRYN SCHULZ

• • •

Shame

"Make it a rule of life never to regret and never to look back. Regret is an appalling waste of energy; you can't build on it; it's only good for wallowing in."
—Katherine Mansfield

• • •

"There are two kinds of guilt: the kind that drowns you until you're useless, and the kind that fires your soul to purpose."
—Sabaa Tahir

• • •

"You can't regret the life you didn't lead."
—JUNOT DÍAZ

● ● ●

"Don't live your life regretting yesterday.
Live your life so tomorrow you won't regret today."
—CATHERINE PULSIFER

● ● ●

"Regret is a universal emotion. We all make wrong
or foolish choices, or something or someone does
something hurtful to us, and we regret it."
—Dave Ferguson

● ● ●

XVI.

∂●

Waiting

Nursing, like all professions, is a series of milestones and waits. You pass an exam and wait. You pass a nursing technique and wait for the next challenge. Each class, each exam will move you forward, but there will be periods of waiting and reflection. Waiting will allow you the opportunity to see where you are and where you want to be. Oftentimes, we are solely focused on the end result, the final goal. So much so that we never appreciate the pause, the wait of each step, each encounter. You passing an exam is a big deal. You passing a prerequisite course is a huge event. These are not simply steps on a ladder—they are your story. And each one will build upon itself, expanding your knowledge base and experience compilation. One piece of advice I give to all nursing professionals is to enjoy the wait and allow yourself time of celebrate.

Don't hold back, saying you will celebrate at the end. The waiting is what keeps you going, what will motivate you in times of desperation and stress. Whether you pass or fail an exam, reflect on the experience. What did you get right? What do you need to work on? What mistakes did you make? What could you have done better? These are all waiting moments; moments that will push you if you respect them and give yourself the proper time. So many people rush through these waiting timelines that they never grow from their experiences. They simply move from one item to the next, like a task master. Life shouldn't and doesn't work that way. You don't get to ignore your experiences, hoping what you needed to know will permeate eventually. Education and skills don't work in that manner. They don't occur simply because time has passed. They have to occur actively and with intention. Don't skip the wait. Understand and respect the wait. Just sit in it and be okay with just being.

"You usually have to wait for that which is worth waiting for."
—CRAIG BRUCE

• • •

"Somewhere, something incredible is waiting to be known."
—SHARON BEGLEY

• • •

"Patience is not simply the ability to wait—
it's how we behave while we're waiting."
—JOYCE MEYER

• • •

"The universe is full of magical things, patiently
waiting for our wits to grow sharper."
—EDEN PHILLPOTTS

• • •

"The best things in life are often waiting for you at the exit ramp of your comfort zone."
—KAREN SALMANSOHN

• • •

"The opposite of talking isn't listening.
The opposite of talking is waiting."
—FRAN LEBOWITZ

• • •

"People are stubborn about what they perceive to be the right thing or the wrong thing, and it takes a long time to filter this human condition. There's a waiting period until people catch up. But if you have patience—which it takes when someone thinks differently from you—everybody always catches up. That patience is a wonderful virtue."
—JOHNNY MATHIS

• • •

"Waiting is painful. Forgetting is painful.
But not knowing which to do is the worse kind of suffering."
—PAULO COELHO

• • •

"Don't become too preoccupied with what is happening around
you. Pay more attention to what is going on within you."
—MARY-FRANCES WINTERS

• • •

"Without reflection, we go blindly on our way, creating more
unintended consequences, and failing to achieve anything useful."
—MARGARET WHEATLEY

• • •

XVII.

፨

Family

I am a person with a fragmented yet close family. Family, to me, isn't simply related to blood ties. My family can and does involve a close circle of friends and colleagues. There are some people I trust more than my own family. I've built a network of people who have earned my trust and friendship, which is why I use the term *family*. I've heard many individuals speak of calling coworkers or colleagues "family" as a bad idea because it creates a toxic environment. I disagree with this statement. Yes, there is a concern in having work relationships, as you are more inclined to tolerate foolishness for the sake of connections. But you need a support system at work; that I know to be true. I work fourteen shifts per month. I interact with some people (some colleagues) more than I do my own grandmother. Those relationships have to be positive and beneficiary to both parties. The title of "family" isn't an all-or-nothing connection. You shouldn't allow anything like toxic behavior, just for the sake of connection.

Family is about trust, and with the number of hours together and the teamwork required, trust must be present in the parties involved. Do I consider every person I encounter at my job to be "family"? Of course not, but I have a select few that I know, if hard times occur or I need to lean on someone, they are there and have earned my trust. It's okay to admit that you need people. This profession is about human connection and trust. Why would that not be a component with the nurses themselves? It's not about favors, manipulation, or cohesion. It's about honest human connection and the shared experience. It is that shared experience that you form trust with. Don't force it—connections occur when it's time and they are genuine. Bonds are created from strength, with each providing their own unique contributions. Family is about the strength those connections provide, not last names or blood lines.

"Coming together is a beginning; keeping together is progress; working together is success."
—Henry Ford

• • •

"Your work is going to fill a large part of your life, and the only way to be truly satisfied is to do what you believe is great work. And the only way to do great work is to love what you do. If you haven't found it yet, keep looking. Don't settle. As with all matters of the heart, you'll know when you find it."
—Steve Jobs

• • •

"Family and work. Family and work. I can let them be at war, with guilt as their nuclear weapon and mutually assured destruction as their aim, or I can let them nourish each other."
—Ellen Gilchrist

• • •

"Don't confuse having a career with having a life."
—Hillary Clinton

• • •

"You don't have to make yourself miserable to be successful. It's natural to look back and mythologize the long nights and manic moments of genius, but success isn't about working hard, it's about working smart."
—ANDREW WILKINSON

• • •

"You will never feel truly satisfied by work until you are satisfied by life."
—HEATHER SCHUCK

• • •

"Call it a clan, call it a network, call it a tribe, call it a family: Whatever you call it, whoever you are, you need one."
—JANE HOWARD

• • •

"The bond that links your true family is not one of blood, but of respect and joy in each other's life."
—RICHARD BACH

• • •

"The strength of a family, like the strength of an army, lies in its loyalty to each other."
—MARIO PUZO

• • •

"When everything goes to hell, the people who stand by you without flinching—they are your family."
—JIM BUTCHER

• • •

XVIII.

Happiness

Are you happy in your current position? This is a question I ask myself every six months or so to gauge whether it's time for a professional change. The nursing profession can be a short or long one. I've known nurses who have been in the profession for thirty-plus years, while others were in the profession for fewer than six months. Every individual has his or her breaking point and will determine his or her own happiness. I personally don't think a certain job or position will make you happy. I didn't get into nursing because I wanted a certain level of income. I wanted to help people. Right now, I am happy, and my passion and skills are matched and appreciated. But as time and work dynamics change, this contentment could transform. Happiness and satisfaction aren't stagnant. They are on a spectrum with change occurring based on your experiences and overall professional criticism. Happiness is on a timeline, and like time it moves, and we move and mature with it.

You are allowed to be happy for years, and suddenly, what you want changes. And therefore, your happiness is redirected and recalculated. Don't let a title hold you back from finding what will make you happy. Titles and positions serve their purpose, but sometimes you outgrow them. Currently, critical care is feeding my soul. I love it, but if further down the road it is not fulfilling me or my needs, I will seek happiness by other means. As my family grows, my needs expand. If certain needs can't be met, I will have decisions to make. I'm comfortable with growth and I fully understand a person's needs to develop as their lives change. You should have management who, too, understands these things. If you don't, know that you don't need to justify your lack of happiness in a certain position to anyone. Just find what makes you happy and go from there.

"Action may not always bring happiness,
but there is no happiness without action."
—BENJAMIN DESRAELI

• • •

"Success is liking yourself, liking what you do,
and liking how you do it."
—MAYA ANGELOU

• • •

"If you want to be happy, set a goal that commands your
thoughts, liberates your energy, and inspires your hopes."
—ANDREW CARNEGIE

• • •

"One of the huge mistakes people make is that they try to force an interest on themselves. You don't choose your passions; your passions choose you."
—JEFF BEZOS

• • •

"Remembering that you are going to die is the best way I know to avoid the trap of thinking you have something to lose. You are already naked. There is no reason not to follow your heart."
—STEVE JOBS

• • •

"When one door of happiness closes, another opens, but often we look so long at the closed door that we do not see the one that has been opened for us."
—HELEN KELLER

• • •

"Even if you are on the right track,
you'll get run over if you just sit there."
—WILL ROGERS

● ● ●

"You don't have to see the whole staircase, just take the first step."
—MARTIN LUTHER KING, JR.

● ● ●

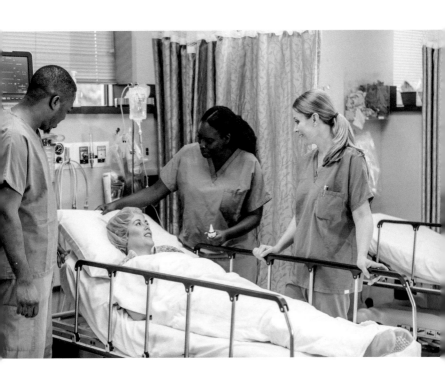

"Happiness is the real sense of fulfillment
that comes from hard work."
—Joseph Barbara

● ● ●

"In a moment of decision, the best thing you can do is the
right thing to do, the next best thing is the wrong thing,
and the worst thing you can do is nothing."
—Theodore Roosevelt

● ● ●

XIX.

Respect

Nursing is one of the most trusted professions year after year. And yet, the respect is lacking (in my opinion) across many levels. I can only speak to my experiences, but I've seen patients as well as medical professionals yell and degrade nurses time and time again. You could say, yes, the medical field creates these circumstances. But we are all adults, and we are all in charge of our reactions and inactions. Each shift, each encounter, I am faced with choices. I choose to respect my team members and understand that my thought processes might vary from theirs. Education and collaboration are key in terms of teamwork. But do not allow someone to disrespect you or your role within the team. I don't like confrontation myself, but I've learned that what we allow will continue. How we allow others to speak to us will form a trend and will be a pattern that is harder to break further down the road. Speak up early, you will be better off. Your role as a nurse involves many things, being a doormat isn't one of them.

For all the new nurses out there, understand that your lack of exposure doesn't equal uselessness or laziness. You are learning, and it's not fair for others to judge you, as most of them have been in their positions for years. These said experiences have allowed them to cultivate their craft and see things you haven't. It's not a fair comparison, so don't make it. Ever! Don't compare your beginning to someone's end. You are not a speed bump or a roadblock. You are a team member, and if you feel you are not being treated that way, speak up and inquire about the root cause. When I'm being yelled at, I say the following: "This type of behavior isn't needed in order to get your point across. Let's remain professional and focus on caring for the patient." That usually snaps people back in line, reminding them of where they are and who they are talking to. You are not a punching bag; you do not deserve to be berated because someone can't process their feelings like an adult.

"Respect your efforts, respect yourself. Self-respect leads to self-discipline. When you have both firmly under your belt, that's real power."
—CLINT EASTWOOD

• • •

"Every human being, of whatever origin, of whatever station, deserves respect. We must each respect others even as we respect ourselves."
—RALPH WALDO EMERSON

• • •

"Respect is an appreciation of the separateness of the other person, of the ways in which he or she is unique."
—ANNIE GOTTLIEB

• • •

"One of the most sincere forms of respect is actually listening to what another has to say."
—BRYANT H. MCGILL

• • •

"Never take a person's dignity:
it is worth everything to them, and nothing to you."
— FRANK BARRON

• • •

"I'm not concerned with your liking or disliking me. . . .
All I ask is that you respect me as a human being."
—JACKIE ROBINSON

• • •

"That you may retain your self-respect, it is better to displease
the people by doing what you know is right, than to temporarily
please them by doing what you know is wrong."
—WILLIAM J. H. BOETCKER

• • •

"I believe that working with good people matters because then the work environment is good. If there is a sense of respect and belief among the people you work with, that is when good work is done."

—Ranbir Kapoor

• • •

"Openness, respect, integrity—these are principles that need to underpin pretty much every other decision that you make."

—Justin Trudeau

• • •

"Different people have different opinions, and it's okay to respect all of them."

—Juan Pablo Galavis

• • •

XX.

Transition

In your career, regardless of track or position, there will be a series of transitions. Whether you go from bedside to management, or medical-surgical to intensive care, you will probably move throughout your organization as your professional skills develop. Searching for your passion isn't something to feel shameful about. You can love nursing and not quite know where or how you want to contribute within the field. You don't need to have an exact plan when you enter the nursing profession, in my opinion. You can walk right in understanding you want to help your community but without knowing exactly how that will be done. I had some colleagues who went from bedside to informatics, and some who went from bedside to leadership. I even had some that fell in love with bedside and remained there until they retired. Everyone's journey is different, and everyone has different goals and passions. What makes me happy will differ from what makes you happy, and that difference shouldn't be judged or interpreted to be anything other than choice. You don't need to explain or elaborate on why you find a certain element of nursing to be interesting or your passion. Just go toward it as fast as you can and with an open heart.

So many people ask me how I still love working in the acute care setting, even after over a decade. And I never have anything else to say other than, "I like it." I enjoy the chaos that is the intensive care setting, with the loud sounds, code blues, unpredictable nights, and intense moments. I can't explain why, though. One day I stopped and realized how freeing it was to just state your feelings without analysis. I don't have to explain why I have a passion for critical care. I don't have to explain why I enjoy working nights. Those are my preferences, and I walked toward them and found a job that provides me with exactly what I was seeking professionally. If your tastes aren't traditional, that's okay too. Nursing is unique in that it has many tracks and lanes, and if you can't find what you are looking for, you might be able to make your own path. I know of many nursing professionals who opened their own businesses. In nursing, you don't settle, you just keep searching, and the journey to find your passion shouldn't be judged or criticized.

"The truth is that our finest moments are most likely to occur when we are feeling deeply uncomfortable, unhappy, or unfulfilled. For it is only in such moments, propelled by our discomfort, that we are likely to step out of our ruts and start searching for different ways or truer answers."
—M. Scott Peck

• • •

"The most difficult thing is the decision to act, the rest is merely tenacity. The fears are paper tigers. You can do anything you decide to do. You can act to change and control your life; and the procedure, the process is its own reward."
—Amelia Earhart

• • •

"In a chronically leaking boat, energy devoted to changing vessels is more productive than energy devoted to patching leaks."
—Warren Buffett

• • •

"There is only one way to avoid criticism: Do nothing, say
nothing, and be nothing."
—ARISTOTLE

• • •

"It is not as much about who you used to be,
as it is about who you choose to be."
—SANHITA BARUAH

• • •

"The most common way people give up their power is by
thinking they don't have any."
—ALICE WALKER

• • •

"Find out what you like doing best,
and get someone to pay you for it."
—Katharine Whitehorn

• • •

"If opportunity doesn't knock, build a door."
—MILTON BERLE

• • •

"I am only one, but I am one. I cannot do everything, but I can do something. I will not let what I cannot do interfere with what I can do."
—EDWARD EVERETT HALE

• • •

"Any fact facing us is not as important as our attitude toward it, for that determines our success or failure."
—NORMAN VINCENT PEALE

• • •

XXI.

Positivity

Nursing, heck the medical profession in general, isn't known for its positivity. Now don't get me wrong, the birth of a baby will always bring a smile to anyone's face. But what I'm talking about is the day-to-day stuff. The illness, the emergency room visits, the death; all will weigh on you. The weight, if not managed properly, can change you. I remember starting out as a graduate nurse and, after a year, I had this negativity within me. I'd come in and do my job but that lightness I once had was gone. The many interactions with bad outcomes changed my perspective and I didn't even see the change. It wasn't until I was talking to my non-nurse friend that she mentioned the change in my personality. "Do you even like being a nurse, still?" she said. I looked at her so confused because I loved being a nurse. Why would she even ask that? "Because you're always complaining. I wasn't sure if you even liked it anymore," she said. Right then I knew I had to really process what was going on.

Instead of assuming my day was going to be miserable and filled with sadness, I changed things up. Each shift, I made a goal and it had to be a positive one. Whether I played my patient's favorite song while giving him or her a bath or listened to a patient tell me about his or her grandkids, at the end of each shift, I purposely made sure I had a positive memory to take home with me. You'd be surprised how easy it is to focus on the negative. Yes, bad things happen, and annoying things happen, too. But there are some good things sprinkled in there, and you might miss them if you only focus on a negative stuff. No one wants to be around someone who constantly complains; their negativity seeps into and latches onto you. I didn't want to be that person, and I didn't want to isolate myself from great, memorable experiences. You are what you put into this career; there isn't a magic button. Patients share their stories, their lives with you, and if you're lucky, you will appreciate these moments and won't overlook how valuable they are.

"Be positive. Be true. Be kind."
—Roy T. Bennett

● ● ●

"If you are positive, you'll see opportunities instead of obstacles."
—Widad Akrawi

● ● ●

"The joy of life comes from our encounters with new experiences,
and hence there is no greater joy than to have an endlessly
changing horizon, for each day to have a new and different sun."
—Christopher McCandless

● ● ●

"If you have a positive attitude and constantly strive to give your best effort, eventually you will overcome your immediate problems and find you are ready for greater challenges."
—PAT RILEY

• • •

"Your attitude is like a box of crayons that color your world. Constantly color your picture gray, and your picture will always be bleak. Try adding some bright colors to the picture by including humor, and your picture begins to lighten up."
—ALLEN KLEIN

• • •

"It takes but one positive thought when given a chance to survive and thrive to overpower an entire army of negative thoughts."
—ROBERT H. SCHULLER

• • •

"Every day brings new choices."
—MARTHA BECK

• • •

"Be thankful for what you have; you'll end up having more. If you concentrate on what you don't have, you will never, ever have enough."
—OPRAH WINFREY

• • •

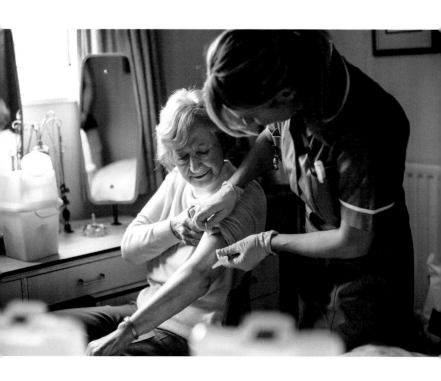

"It will never rain roses: when we want to have more roses, we must plant more roses."
—George Eliot

• • •

"People tend to be generous when sharing their nonsense, fear, and ignorance. And while they seem quite eager to feed you their negativity, please remember that sometimes the diet we need to be on is a spiritual and emotional one. Be cautious with what you feed your mind and soul. Fuel yourself with positivity and let that fuel propel you into positive action."
—Steve Maraboli

• • •

XXII.

Colleagues

As a nurse, we interact with all types from people from all different walks of life. We don't get to pick our assignments. We take care of all folks regardless of history and conditions. Same goes for our colleagues. We work with all types of people from all backgrounds. Nursing was where I was educated about the Egyptian culture by a nurse from Cairo. I had pancit for the first time when a Filipino nurse brought it to a potluck. When you allow yourself to learn from the others around you, you expand your outlook and perspective on so many topics. Little ol' me was just a country girl from Kissimmee, Florida. But nursing brought a cast of amazing, cultured, worldly people into my life. Each and every one of them taught me something from their culture, and I used that knowledge in my professional and personal life. As a bedside nurse, my hospital had an amazing international nursing program. Every couple of months, nurses from all over the world would come and work with us. We had nurses from the Philippines, India, and other countries.

Understand that work isn't simply about performing tasks. You interact with patients, but more importantly, you have the opportunity to learn from the colleagues around you—doctors, nurses, technologists, therapists, nutritionists, leadership—about everything from vasopressors, ventilator settings, and tube feedings to the best place to get a good burger at 7 a.m. Don't simply pass by the people you spend the most time with. Learn from them, pick their brains. Learn from the experienced nurses around you; they always have tricks and know who to call and when. Learn from the respiratory therapists, about the different ventilator modes and breathing treatments. Learn from leadership, about upcoming projects or departmental needs. There is a wealth of knowledge around you; all you have to do is step forward and start the conversation. Keeping your head down is great in theory, but nursing is a team effort. No one person is responsible for everything and no one person can do it all. Sharing your story with others allows them to share theirs with you.

"Talent wins games, but teamwork and
intelligence win championships."
—MICHAEL JORDAN

• • •

"When I speak with people who love their jobs and have
vital friendships at work, they always talk about how their
workgroup is like a family."
—TOM RATH

• • •

"Motivation comes from working on things we care about.
It also comes from working with people we care about."
—SHERYL SANDBERG

• • •

"A good life depends on the strength of our relationships with family, friends, neighbors, colleagues and strangers."
—DAVID LAMMY

• • •

"You can't change the world alone—you will need some help—and to truly get from your starting point to your destination takes friends, colleagues, the good will of strangers and a strong coxswain to guide them."
—WILLIAM H. MCRAVEN

• • •

"Finding your soul begins by discovering our ability to listen! Alternatively, by sharing a smile, a laugh and just by being human to everyone—from friends, colleagues, family, and especially strangers, including those who are not from the same station in life as you."
—OM MALIK

• • •

"I'm not the smartest fellow in the world,
but I can sure pick smart colleagues."
—Franklin D. Roosevelt

• • •

"Instead of turning away from our neighbors, our friends, our
colleagues, let us instead learn from our history and avoid
repeating the mistakes of our past."
—Loretta Lynch

• • •

"If you're not making use of even the most routine
assignment to learn something, realize that many
of your colleagues and coworkers are."
—Adena Friedman

• • •

"Treat employees like partners, and they act like partners."
—Fred Allen

• • •

XXIII.

Practice

Nursing involves a ton of critical thinking and practice, along with technique. Technique is how one nurse can "feel" a vein when another nurse can't seem to locate a juicy one for an IV line. Practice doesn't make perfect—perfect makes perfect. And understand that perfecting your craft will take time. In that journey, you will make mistakes and have a few errors. For example, I almost failed my insulin technique check-off in nursing school. It wasn't because I didn't know how to perform the technique; it was because I was nervous and froze. Freezing happens. Everyone talks about action, in terms of making a mistake. My mind simply stopped working, and I just forgot all the many hours of studying I had completed the day prior. It wasn't until a classmate told me to repeat the action until I no longer had to think about it that I learned the importance of practice. Practice isn't sexy or cool; it's boring but an oh-so-necessary part of the educational process.

You are not Jason Bourne; you will not know how to perform under pressure automatically. This isn't a movie, it's life. If you want to tap into a skill, you have to practice it for improvement. No nursing professional starts out an expert at a task or technique. Remember your first indwelling catheter insertion (in a female)? Yeah, not like the mannequin, right? It's only until you do it a few times that you know what to look for and the anatomical landmarks on actual human beings. Everything is like that. You can read all day, but until you act upon the knowledge you have absorbed, it won't come to you. With that in mind, I recommend you take every opportunity to practice whatever skills you want to perfect. Don't wait, don't be passive. Be active in your skillset cultivation and elevation. Moving toward an unknown skill is terrifying—I'm not going to lie to you. But experience is unmatched, and it's better to improve in times of calm rather than in intense, scary situations. Who would want to learn how to insert an IV during a code blue when there is no other current IV access? Not me.

"Take chances, make mistakes. That's how you grow.
Pain nourishes your courage. You have to fail in order
to practice being brave."
—Mary Tyler Moore

• • •

"Knowledge is of no value unless you put it into practice."
—Anton Chekhov

• • •

"The more you practice and study, the better you are . . .
so I still practice and study all the time."
—Cyndi Lauper

• • •

"People believe practice makes perfect, but it doesn't. If you're making a tremendous amount of mistakes, all you're doing is deeply ingraining the same mistakes."
—JILLIAN MICHAELS

• • •

"I'm a strong believer that you practice like you play, little things make big things happen."
—TONY DORSETT

• • •

"Through practice, gently and gradually we can collect ourselves and learn how to be more fully with what we do."
—JACK KORNFIELD

• • •

"Practice means to perform, over and over again in the face of all obstacles, some act of vision, of faith, of desire. Practice is a means of inviting the perfection desired."
—MARTHA GRAHAM

• • •

"Practice is the hardest part of learning, and training is the essence of transformation."
—ANN VOSKAMP

• • •

"We, in fact, determine how skilled we become in the sense that if we choose not to practice, we recognize that we will not move beyond the point at which we stopped."
—BYRON PULSIFER

• • •

"One of the paradoxes of life is that being impatient often makes it harder to achieve something. As with any skill, you get better at manifesting the more you practice."
—SIMON FOSTER

• • •

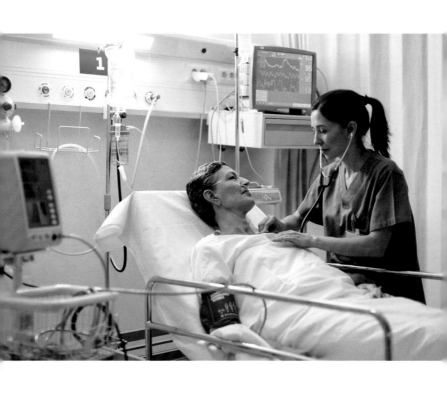

XXIV.

ॐ

Control

One definition of control is to determine the behavior or supervise the running of something. In healthcare, we advocate for our patients, and that includes their decisions. The decisions, if they line up with your way of thinking, are very easy to advocate for, as we understand their pathway. The issue comes when you don't understand a decision from a patient, and how you manage those feelings. Whether a patient is refusing a certain treatment that could save their life, or they are prolonging a process you find to be futile, you will have to reconcile how you feel about things. You have to accept that you have no control over what your patients choose to do or not do with the information they are given. Refusing blood products in the midst of hemorrhagic shock seems illogical. But speak to a Jehovah's Witness about their choice, and they will explain the religious commitments tied to that decision. It isn't simply about the intervention, it's the connections and implications of the intervention. It's deeper and more complex.

You, as a caregiver, can provide all the education and evidence-based research tied to a recommendation, intervention, or decision. And your patients may still make a decision you find difficult or troubling to accept. You have no control over what your patients decide and how they come to conclusions regarding what they will and will not accept. We, as caregivers, only provide the most truthful, factual information and that is it. We present and await their choice. That lack of control can be frustrating, but that's life. Who's to say you are right or the patient is right? This isn't a contest, and you don't get points for proving someone wrong. As humans, our decision-making process is influenced by tons of things, including past experiences, cultural influences, and childhood principles. We don't get to negate or minimize someone's cultural background because we can't understand it or have no reference point. You must accept that control will always be limited, accept that you are not in charge.

"You must learn to let go. Release the stress.
You were never in control anyway."
—STEVE MARABOLI

• • •

"You cannot control what happens to you, but you can control
your attitude toward what happens to you, and in that, you will
be mastering change rather than allowing it to master you."
—BRIAN TRACY

• • •

"The only thing you sometimes have control over is perspective.
You don't have control over your situation. But you have a choice
about how you view it."
—CHRIS PINE

• • •

"A lot of things are going to happen that you can't necessarily control all the time, but you can control what you do after it happens. So that's what I try to do, keep my head up, keep moving forward, stay positive and just work hard."
—LONZO BALL

• • •

"Being in control of your life and having realistic expectations about your day-to-day challenges are the keys to stress management, which is perhaps the most important ingredient to living a happy, healthy and rewarding life."
—MARILU HENNER

• • •

"At the end of the day, you can't control the results; you can only control your effort level and your focus."
—BEN ZOBRIST

• • •

"I don't have any control over what actually happens except for that I have full control over my will for myself, my intention, and why I'm there. That's all that matters."

—SZA

• • •

"What we can control is our performance and our execution, and that's what we're going to focus on."

—Bill Belichick

• • •

"Everything happens kind of the way it's supposed to happen, and we just watch it unfold. And you can't control it. Looking back, you can't say, 'I should've . . .' You didn't, and had you, the outcome would have been different."

—Rick Rubin

• • •

"You can control two things: your work ethic and your attitude about anything."

—Ali Krieger

• • •

XXV.

Appreciate

My dad would always tell me to appreciate certain moments. As a teenager, I wanted nothing more than the time to move faster, and those moments to be erased and forgotten. Now as a nurse, I understand how important the mediocrity is. When my kids wake up and I see them smile and say good morning, or when my husband is eating cereal and he hums a song—it's the little things that make the big moments. And it's the same in healthcare. Yes, saving someone's life is amazing, but so is feeding a patient or listening to them talk about their grandkids. It's all about appreciating who loves you and what you love in the end. Nursing has its rough moments. From short staffing to limited supplies, a 12-hour shift can quickly feel like a 196-hour shift. In all the chaos and unpredictability that is the world, take the time to appreciate the good things you have and hold on to them. Because they and you won't and don't last forever.

Appreciate good outcomes and patients being discharged from the hospital. Appreciate a fully staffed floor, you being able to eat lunch and peeing when you want. Happiness shouldn't only be during grand gestures and when epic things happen. What about you passing an exam? Or taking your kids to the pool? Those moments are the meat and potatoes of life; don't let the vegetable medley (the bad things) distract you. Distraction is our downfall. Nursing school is all about the next test, the next check-off, the next course. I understand the focus required to get through it. I had about five nervous breakdowns in nursing school, haha. But once you reach your goal of being a nurse, you have to expand your focus and appreciate what is around you, your environment, your air. No one appreciates their health until they are ill. I didn't appreciate or understand the complexity of fertility until I had my own ten-year battle. Moments, time, experiences, and emotions are all we have. Treat them with respect.

"Life is NOT short! It's just by the time we catch up to appreciating
it . . . we've already left life at least halfway behind us."
—Sanjo Jendayi

• • •

"Sometimes in life we need to sit with things for a minute,
maybe on the fringe of things, not only to savor the
wealth of the moment, but take a moment to figure out
how to respectfully engage it."
—Craig D. Lounsbrough

• • •

"Appreciate and don't take for granted the things and people you
have. Better yet take the good out of the situations you may face."
—Hopal Green

• • •

". . . If you don't read the middle, you can't appreciate
how beautiful the ending really is."
—S.C. MONSON

• • •

"Don't fight for what you don't have, fight for what you have."
—DOUW PRINSLOO

• • •

"Appreciation is the highest form of prayer, for it acknowledges
the presence of good wherever you shine the light of your
thankful thoughts."
—ALAN COHEN

• • •

"I may not be where I want to be but I'm thankful
for not being where I used to be."
—HABEEB AKANDE

• • •

"Unhappiness is a contagious disease caused
by a chronic deficiency of gratitude."
—MOKOKOMA MOKHONOANA

• • •

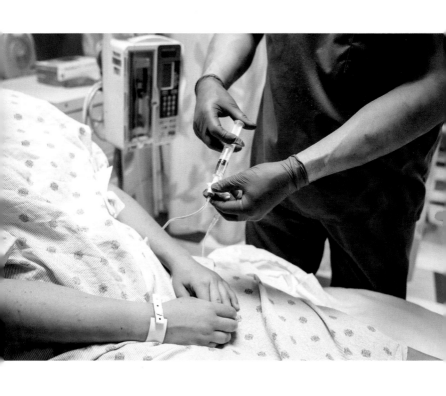

"Now is no time to think of what you do not have.
Think of what you can do with what there is."
—ERNEST HEMINGWAY

• • •

"It is necessary, then, to cultivate the habit of being grateful
for every good thing that comes to you, and to give thanks
continuously. And because all things have contributed to your
advancement, you should include all things in your gratitude."
—WALLACE D. WATTLES

• • •

XXVI.

୬●

Machine

Think of a task you have to perform in your shift, let's say administering medication. Now, most nurses would picture, perhaps a nurse giving a patient medication. Cut and dried, right? But that one act is an accumulation of many acts. From the manufacturer, to transport, to pharmacy, to medication delivery, to placement in the medication dispensary machine, to you. That one task has many moving parts in order for you to provide your patient with what he or she needs. Keep that same thought process in mind when it comes to all the care you provide. You ever run out of normal saline flushes during a shift? Or clean washcloths? I have, and I used to get frustrated because how are we out of these things? It wasn't until my manager told me that every floor has levels, counts, related costs, and inventory requirements that I understood how complicated simply keeping a stock accurate could be. We, as individuals, have no control over a big organization's decision to stock or not stock something. I can advocate a need for a certain item and inform management. But getting all hot and bothered about something I have no control over only hurts me and my focus.

I can't control how my organization processes bills for patients. I can't control if a provider orders a certain medication. All I can do is advocate, perform, and ensure my actions are professional, safe, and in line with my organization's goals. When you work for big organizations, sometimes the politics can get the best of you, which leads people to focus on the wrong things. The only things you have control over are your perspective and actions. We are all moving parts in a machine, a machine that helps our community. But you don't have control over aspects you are not a part of or lack input in changing. As a nurse, I have no control over when radiology calls for upcoming imaging. All I can do is inform the team that the patient and I are ready for transport and that's it. I also have no control over when nutrition trays are delivered. Getting all upset about them being late only causes me emotional distress and distraction. No one else. If you want change, you have to speak up. But understand that what you say may or may not prompt others to act. And that is okay. What is not okay is getting stressed and overwhelmed about outer workings of multiple processes that are outside of your control.

"Communication works for those who work at it."
—JOHN POWELL

• • •

"People become attached to their burdens sometimes
more than the burdens are attached to them."
—GEORGE BERNARD SHAW

• • •

"The truth is that stress doesn't come from your boss,
your kids, your spouse, traffic jams, health challenges,
or other circumstances. It comes from your thoughts
about your circumstances."
—ANDREW BERNSTEIN

• • •

"It isn't the mountain ahead that wears you out;
it's the grain of sand in your shoe."
—ROBERT W. SERVICE

• • •

"Our anxiety does not come from thinking about the future,
but from wanting to control it."
—KAHLIL GIBRAN

• • •

"There are some people who always seem angry and continuously
look for conflict. Walk away from these people. The battle they
are fighting isn't with you, it's with themselves."
—RASHIDA ROWE

• • •

"One of the best ways to reduce stress is to accept
the things that you cannot control."
—M. P. NEARY

• • •

"Sometimes we can focus so much on nothing that
we make it a big something of nothing."
—RICKY MAYE

• • •

"Remember that stress doesn't come from what's going
on in your life. It comes from your thoughts about
what's going on in your life."
—ANDREW BERNSTEIN

• • •

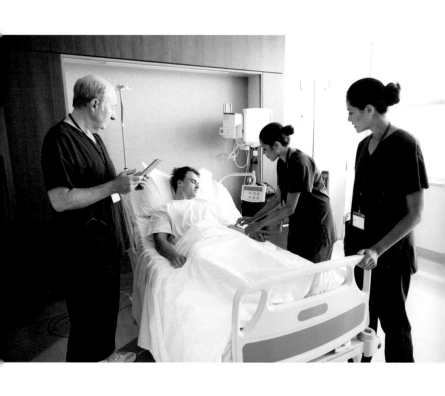

XXVII.

Welcome

Each shift brings an adventure. Whether you work in outpatient or inpatient, each patient will be a new experience. I've been a nurse for more than ten years, and sepsis doesn't ever present itself the same way. Disease processes are learned in nursing school and management is perfected on the job. I can articulate what sepsis or hyperglycemia should present as. But in terms of actual presentation, the body can surprise you. The patient's compensatory mechanisms and medical background will cause disease processes to present differently than expected. The textbook is a guide, but don't assume all the checkboxes will be checked and applicable. This is why being a graduate nurse is so difficult in the beginning. What you are taught might not necessarily be present. This is why the first year of nursing can be the most difficult in terms of adjusting. I remember being a student and being frustrated, as what I saw wasn't necessarily what I learned. My preceptor then said, "Welcome to real-world nursing."

You can read all the books you want. You must understand patients come with a level of unpredictability in terms of their disease process. Not everyone will respond to antibiotics or mechanical ventilation. You are dealing with years and years of medical history and a body that has gone through a lot. A mild disease can overwhelm some patients, to the point of death. Our textbooks don't even explain that aspect of care. Textbooks provide care plans, management, and outcomes. I remember when I had my first end-stage congestive heart failure patient; I couldn't wrap my mind around the heart failure leading to someone's death. There are so many medications out there and interventions available. It wasn't until a cardiologist explained how the body is one big machine and sometimes the parts don't work as well as they should—that I understood. The damaged parts can cause other issues, and other parts become damaged as a result. Body systems don't work in silos; they all work and react together. The real world is your welcome into understanding the cascading effects of the human condition, understanding that not all conditions are treatable and not all outcomes will be positive.

"By three methods we may learn wisdom: First, by reflection, which is noblest; Second, by imitation, which is easiest; and third by experience, which is the bitterest."
—CONFUCIUS

• • •

"Nothing ever becomes real 'til it is experienced."
—JOHN KEATS

• • •

"If you want to know the taste of a pear, you must change the pear by eating it yourself. If you want to know the theory and methods of revolution, you must take part in revolution. All genuine knowledge originates in direct experience."
—Mao Zedong

• • •

"Face reality as it is, not as it was or as you wish it to be."
—Jack Welch

• • •

"Thinking something does not make it true.
Wanting something does not make it real."
—Michelle Hodkin

• • •

"Real life is only ever just real life. Messy.
What it means depends on how you look at it. The only
thing you've got to do is find a way to live there."
—PATRICK NESS

• • •

"Information is not knowledge. The only source of knowledge is
experience. You need experience to gain wisdom."
—Albert Einstein

• • •

"Knowledge gained through experience is far superior and many times more useful than bookish knowledge."
—MAHATMA GANDHI

● ● ●

"There can be no doubt that all our knowledge begins with experience."
—IMMANUEL KANT

● ● ●

"Whatever your goal in life, the beginning is knowledge and experience."
—HENRY FORD

● ● ●

XXVIII.

ॐ

Relationships

I wish, when I was a nursing student, someone had explained to me that I would be an audience for the many relationships with my community. When you care for someone who is critically ill, family and loved ones will come for updates and information. You'd think it would be pretty straightforward, but sometimes it isn't. Husbands who are sick will be visited by their wives and, also, their girlfriends. Partners will come to visit their loved one and meet another person *also* in a relationship with their loved one. A big family of five-plus siblings will arrive to the bedside and as a team and must work together. You can't get five people to order lunch in thirty minutes, let alone five people to agree on a plan and have no qualms or doubts about their decisions. We aren't talking about what the fastest route is to the airport, we are talking about serious decisions, end-of-life decisions. And if these relationships are strained, fractured, or weak, those issues will present themselves in your presence. You don't know your patient personally, but these individuals will provide you with a glimpse into their lives, what they would have wanted, and their choices.

You, luckily, aren't there to fix these issues; you are there to advocate. Make sure the legally appropriate person or persons are able to make the decisions and act accordingly. I don't judge fathers who haven't talked to their kids in years or a wife with a boyfriend on the side. People are complex, history is long and beyond my understanding. A person's actions and choices are theirs to carry. Just advocate, inform, and act when needed. Will it be messy? Perhaps—you are dealing with many unpacked emotions and convoluted dynamics. But don't get caught up is all the drama. Everyone's life has drama and background. Don't judge a person by what you think you know. Keep your focus on the job and help where you can. Don't allow relationships to distract you or alter your decision-making. We advocate and do what is best. All the other stuff is background noise. Be grateful people are present and there to make choices. Sadly, not all patients have this luxury.

"Nothing is perfect. Life is messy. Relationships are complex.
Outcomes are uncertain. People are irrational."
—Pietro Aretino

• • •

"It's hard to communicate anything exactly and that's why perfect
relationships between people are difficult to find."
—Gustave Flaubert

• • •

"Some relationships just move from one
unresolved conflict to another."
—H. Norman Wright

• • •

"Relationships don't always make sense.
Especially from the outside."
—SARAH DESSEN

• • •

"Every relationship is different. Everyone loves differently."
—RICHELLE MEAD

• • •

"All life is part of a complex relationship in which each is
dependent upon the others, taking
from, giving to and living with all the rest."
—JACQUES YVES COUSTEAU

• • •

"Every relationship has fissures and cracks. That doesn't mean it's meaningless or bad or even wrong. We know that everything in our lives is complex and gray. Yet we somehow expect our relationships to never be anything but simple and pure."
—HARLAN COBEN

• • •

"My relationship with him was defined by these complex emotions, this mixture of gratitude and resentment."
—OTSUICHI

• • •

"The human mind is an open network of complex softwares working together."
—SUKANT RATNAKAR

• • •

"Almost nothing is as complex as the human personality, and no simple formula will ever cover every situation or every relationship."
—BILLY GRAHAM

• • •

XXIX.

Feedback

No one likes being wrong; no one likes being corrected. You will get this constantly when you are on the job training to be a nurse and at a desk in class. It's called learning and, along the way, you will trip and stumble. These bumps are expected and aren't a sign of anything. Having issues in your pediatrics class or issues with calculating infusion drip rates doesn't mean you can't be a nurse. It only means you need more practice. Don't get me wrong; nursing is complicated and it has its moments of complexity. But nursing isn't over anyone's head, in my opinion. If you want to help people, you can do it. I hate to sound like a guidance counselor here, but it's true. I've seen too many nurses quit after an issue and move on. It breaks my heart for someone to have a passion for something and decide they "must" give it up after making a mistake. Mistakes will be made; perfection isn't a thing. What *is* a thing is passion, drive, professionalism, and dedication. If you dedicate yourself to developing your skillset, everything else will fall into place. Persistence will get you there.

Back in the day, when someone would provide me feedback, I'd get defensive. I would take their feedback personally and spiral in my own mind about all the things that conversation might have meant. It wasn't until a year into my preceptorship that I realized it was professional criticism and nothing more. Your preceptor is there to judge your performance, to ensure you will be a safe colleague. Don't get caught up in the emotions. Understand the nature of the relationship and accept that you are being evaluated. Always put your best foot forward but know that corrections will be necessary. No one grows up and just knows how to be a nurse. Each floor, each department requires different skills and varying level of focus. Allow you preceptor to educate you on the departmental needs and assist you down your career path. You are not being judged on your personality; you are being judged on performance and contribution efforts.

"Do not let arrogance go to your head and despair to your heart;
do not let compliments go to your head and criticisms to your
heart; do not let success go to your head and failure to your heart."
—ROY T. BENNETT

• • •

"To avoid criticism say nothing, do nothing, be nothing."
—ELBERT HUBBARD

• • •

"Criticism may not be agreeable, but it is necessary.
It fulfils the same function as pain in the human body;
it calls attention to the development of an unhealthy state
of things. If it is heeded in time, danger may be averted;
if it is suppressed, a fatal distemper may develop."
—WINSTON CHURCHILL

• • •

"You can't let praise or criticism get to you. It's a weakness to get caught up in either one."
—JOHN WOODEN

• • •

"Criticism is just someone else's opinion. Even people who are experts in their fields are sometimes wrong. It is up to you to choose whether to believe some of it, none of it, or all of it. What you think is what counts."
—RODOLFO COSTA

• • •

"True intuitive expertise is learned from prolonged experience with good feedback on mistakes."
—DANIEL KAHNEMAN

• • •

"When we make progress and get better at something, it is inherently motivating. In order for people to make progress, they have to get feedback and information on how they're doing."
—Daniel H. Pink

• • •

"Dig for feedback on yourself. You need to have the courage to ask for feedback. You need to learn how you can learn how to grow. It is important that you are going to be a lifelong learner."
—Scott Cook

• • •

"If you don't get feedback from your performers and your audience, you're going to be working in a vacuum."
—Peter Maxwell Davies

• • •

"It's a challenge to grow professionally and move up the corporate ladder when you're not receiving feedback on your performance."
—John Rampton

• • •

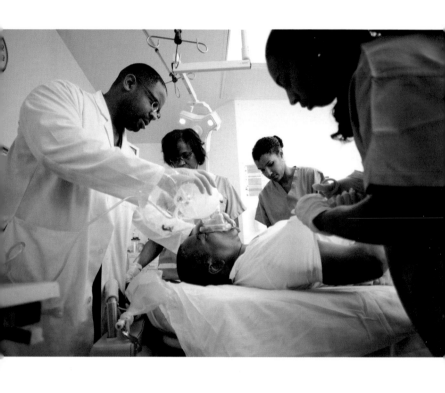

XXX.

Pressure

In the field of nursing, there will moments when pressure is applied to you. Whether you need to complete a task by a certain time or you are put on the spot to explain something, these moments will occur. Pressure is stressful but helpful (when done in the right way). The act of caring for someone is stressful within itself. Pressure can be very motivating and useful in the nursing profession. Pressure is what helped me with my time management. In nursing school, mild pressure is applied during clinical rotations. You are there to learn, not refine any time-management skills. You complete your assignments on time (academically), but during clinical rotations, there were no hard deadlines (from my experience). Then boom, you start your job and have to distribute ten to twelve medications to five patients all in fifteen minutes, in a safe, appropriate fashion. Medication passes are key moments that require all your attention and focus. Yet, you have all these other things on your mind and tons of things you need to do.

The pressure is on for you to perform (safely), for your patients and for your team. I find organization and expectations as ways to ease pressure and allow me the headspace I need to perform successfully. Organization is a boring topic, but without it, you will fail. Your day is in front of you. What's important? What has to be done now? Any time-critical medications? There are levels of importance. Patients must get their scheduled medications and must be present for any procedures ordered. Expectations are another component. What is required of you? Are you meeting the job expectations and objectives? Lack of knowledge exacerbates pressure. If you have no information or context about something, it will be fearful and stressful when you are required to perform that thing. Ask your colleagues for any suggestions or tips, create tools to help improve your performance. Don't see your job as an obstacle course; see it as your opportunity to elevate your greatness. Now, you can't do everything always—you will burn out. I'm talking about making healthy, attainable performance changes so the pressure dissipates.

"Everything negative—pressure, challenges—
is all an opportunity for me to rise."
—Kobe Bryant

• • •

"You have to cherish things in a different way when you
know the clock is ticking, you are under pressure."
—Chadwick Boseman

• • •

"Success doesn't motivate me as much as integrity does. Everyone loses. I enjoy the pressure of showing up every single day, being focused, putting forth my best effort, getting the best out of my teammates, and enjoying the journey."
—BECKY SAUERBRUNN

• • •

"Mistakes and pressure are inevitable; the secret to getting past them is to stay calm."
—TRAVIS BRADBERRY

• • •

"Enjoy the pressure. Enjoy the stress. Enjoy being uncomfortable.
And don't shy away from it, embrace it."
—GARY WOODLAND

• • •

"Pressure is something you feel when you
don't know what you're doing."
—CHUCK NOLL

• • •

"We feel pressure from every angle to meet expectations,
but the pressure also pushes us in a positive way as well."
—MOMO HIRAI

• • •

"Pressure is a privilege."
—Ashleigh Barty

• • •

"'Pressure' is a word that is misused in our vocabulary.
When you start thinking of pressure, it's because
you've started to think of failure."
—Tommy Lasorda

• • •

"Pressure brings the best out of people, or it can bring the worst
out. It's just how you use it."
—Clint Dempsey

• • •

XXXI.

৯•

Culture

"It depends on the culture" is something I've heard time and time again regarding which behaviors are acceptable and what the expectations are. *Culture* is a term often used when people want to lump a group of individuals who respond or act in a certain manner. For example, if a floor is filled with bullies, the culture of that floor is therefore bully-led and bully-accepted. In my opinion, if a group of people are acting a certain way, it means the behavior and, therefore, their actions, have been accepted on some level. Regardless of what anyone says, leadership has on some level either endorsed or ignored the behavior, and ignoring a problem is a form of acceptance (again, in my opinion). Wherever you work, make sure the culture suits you. I've heard of nurses bullying others or floors where mistakes were not accepted. The sad thing is, one person can't change a culture—we can only exist within it. If the culture is toxic, provide feedback but understand that a culture is hard to change alone. Sometimes it easier to move on or walk away if it starts impacting your personal life or emotional space.

I'd love to tell you that anyone can change anything, but it's not true. I worked on a toxic floor once. Each shift was unbearable and anxiety filled. I almost had to go on medication from the level of panic and anxiety just going to work would cause me. Every question was met with snarky remarks and personal attacks. Each person refused to help me and there was no teamwork. Every time I went into work, I knew it was going to be a rough twelve hours. Who wants to do that long term? I love challenges, and I love rising to the occasion and proving people wrong. But I will not allow a job to cause me emotional harm. You don't get an award for emotional distress and anxiety. Emotions and feelings are important and when ignored can cause you and your loved ones a great deal of harm. Emotions can only be compartmentalized for so long until they bleed into other aspects of your life. If needed, seek management advice and guidance. If you feel your concerns fall on deaf ears and nothing is changing, be strong enough to move on. It's not failure, it's growth. It's understanding your worth and your need to find a place or organization that wants to develop your professional skills and create an atmosphere for learning and positivity.

"Performance more often comes down to a cultural challenge,
rather than simply a technical one."
—Lara Hogan

• • •

"Company Culture is the product of a company's values,
expectations, and environment."
—Courtney Chapman

• • •

"Corporate culture matters. How management chooses to treat
its people impacts everything for better or for worse."
—Simon Sinek

• • •

"The culture of a company is the sum of the behaviors
of all its people."
—MICHAEL KOULY

• • •

"Culture is what motivates and retains talented employees."
—BETTY THOMPSON

• • •

"Culture is like the wind. It is invisible;
yet its effect can be seen and felt."
—BRYAN WALKER

• • •

"Employee Engagement arises out of culture and
not the other way around."
—CARRICK AND DUNAWAY

• • •

"A great organizational culture is highlighted by cohesion, collaboration, and compassion."
—EILEEN MCDARGH

• • •

"Organizational culture is a combination of behaviors and attitudes exhibited by leaders and employees across an organization that create the underlying vibe of that company."
—CARA SILLETTO

• • •

"Organizational Culture is creating an environment where people 'want' to go to work, not 'have' to go to work."
—JACK DALY

• • •

XXXII.

Protection

As a nurse, you have a state (or multistate) nursing license. Your actions or inactions can cause you trouble in any given situation. Whether it's a complaint or license suspension, take every decision at work as one that will be scrutinized (as it should). Medical professionals have an immense power and a knowledge advantage over their patients. Nurses are the most trusted professionals year after year. The role must be respected. The license is your key to the greatest profession out there; don't mess it up. This same thought process applies when you are given an assignment. If the assignment is dangerous or unsafe, it is in your best interest to speak up and advocate for yourself. Advocate as well as you would for a patient in need. Because trust me, you need your license. Nursing licenses are an honor, and once you lose your license or get it suspended, it will drastically change your options and impact your life for an extended period of time.

I have a passion for nursing, but I don't allow the passion to blind me to the business of medicine. Some days, you will be short-staffed, and some days you will not have the resources you need. All businesses face these issues from time to time. But when it comes to me being responsible or accepting a situation, I have control over whether I take the responsibility. No one can make you take a dangerous assignment. You, for sure, can't abandon a patient assignment, though, which goes to show you just how serious the entire process is. When you accept an assignment, you accept many things as they are. If you feel uncomfortable with the assignment or feel your skill level doesn't match the assignment, speak up. I spoke up when I was a bedside nurse, and I speak up now as an acute care nurse practitioner. If something is above my scope of practice or its complexity requires additional help, you better believe I'm speaking up. I wouldn't want to cause harm due to my abilities coming up short or due to lack of knowledge. It isn't about ego. It's about protection, for you and for your patient.

"You are your own last line of defense in safety.
It all boils down to you."
—KINA REPP

• • •

"Safety is something that happens between your ears,
not something you hold in your hands."
—JEFF COOPER

• • •

"Deterrence itself is not a preeminent value;
the primary values are safety and morality."
—HERMAN KAHN

• • •

"Safety brings first aid to the uninjured."
—F. S. HUGHES

• • •

"To say nothing is saying something. You must denounce
things you are against or one might believe that
you support things you really do not."
—GERMANY KENT

• • •

"No voice is too soft when that voice speaks for others."
—JANNA CACHOLA

• • •

"All truths are easy to understand once they are discovered;
the point is to discover them."
—GALILEO GALILEI

• • •

"If you don't like it, say something."
—JOYCE RACHELLE

• • •

"When you see something that is not right, not fair, not just, you have
to speak up. You have to say something; you have to do something."
—JOHN LEWIS

• • •

XXXIII.

First Steps

Before I was a nurse, I was in hospitality and retail, with dreams of being a nurse. It wasn't until I was laid off that I finally had the time to dedicate myself to the prerequisite courses required to apply for nursing school. Taking those classes were my first steps. It was scary and difficult, but look where it got me! First steps are always the hardest things to do because you don't know where they are going to take you. Will I fail this class? Will I get into this nursing program? It's all unknown until you try. And yes, like your kindergarten teacher used to say, "Trying is important." No one gives themselves credit for merely taking steps towards their goal. They only focus on the end results and the success of it all. You have to appreciate the courage it took you to even consider a goal and walk toward it. So many people are too scared to even try and put themselves out there to possibly fail. Failure is scary, but inaction is worse.

You won't ever face failure if you attempt nothing. It's easy to give excuses as to why you shouldn't attempt something you have a passion for. You might embarrass yourself or you might waste your time. Both could occur, but what if none occur? What if the opposite happens? When you find your passion, you persist, you dig in and work toward you goal. That dedication and persistence will allow you to reach your goal. I haven't met one person yet who has said nursing was their passion but they never became a nurse. If you're so-so or neutral about nursing, any obstacle or challenge you face will be met with annoyance and lack of effort, as you don't really care about the end goal. But when you have a passion, you do what is needed and take the necessary steps. The passion will drive you, guide you toward your goal. But if you don't take those first steps, that passion remains unused and unmet.

"The first step toward success is taken when you refuse to be a captive of the environment in which you first find yourself."
—Mark Caine

• • •

"The first step towards getting somewhere is to decide that you are not going to stay where you are."
—Chauncey Depew

• • •

"You must take the first step. The first steps will take some effort, maybe pain. But after that, everything that has to be done is real-life movement."
—Ben Stein

• • •

"Take the first step, and your mind will mobilize all its forces to your aid. But the first essential is that you begin. Once the battle is startled, all that is within and without you will come to your assistance."
—ROBERT COLLIER

• • •

"The first step is you have to say that you can."
—WILL SMITH

• • •

"Setting goals is the first step in turning the invisible into the visible."
—TONY ROBBINS

• • •

"Even the greatest was once a beginner.
Don't be afraid to take that first step."
—Muhammad Ali

• • •

"The first step is to believe that it's possible. Once I had a taste of
success, you start to believe in it a little more."
—Jarome Iginla

• • •

"The journey of a thousand miles begins with a single step.
Watch your step."
—Thomas S. Monson

• • •

"Decide that you are not going to stay where you are."
—J. P. Morgan

• • •

XXXIV.

कॐ

Yourself

So many things we look at daily make us doubt who we are, what we want, and what we do. The world is filled with people giving you advice and suggestions. Each minute you receive tons of recommendations from varying outlets. If these things are warranted, great. But don't ever forget that you are amazing exactly the way you are. Life is learning, and it's a forever journey. But that doesn't mean you are undone or incomplete in the process. Smile, appreciate where you are and who are right now. A patient told me once, "I was waiting for this certain time in my life to do what I wanted and be happy. I wish I was doing it all along." This hit home for me because I was one of those people who delayed things until it was the "right" time. I would hyper-focus on one thing and remain in unhealthy situations because the timing was off. Both resulted in me being quasi-happy and holding back what would have made me truly happy. You can be working toward a goal and still go out with your friends and still love exactly where you are in the world. Being miserable until a certain goal is met isn't beneficial.

Yes, reaching a goal you worked hard for is awesome. But don't allow goal setting to make your surroundings toxic and nonnurturing. Negativity is contagious and can bleed into all aspects of your life. If you are on a learning journey, appreciate what you've accomplished and what you are working toward. A goal is the end point, but the journey is the adventure. The journey isn't to be a negative experience filled with tension. Who wants to live in that state for a long period of time? You are pending greatness, but the pending doesn't mean you have to be miserable. Your value isn't determined by how many goals you reached or worked toward. Your identity isn't defined by a goal either. You are awesome solo. Self-acceptance and self-love are necessary. Appreciate your hard work, celebrate the little victories; it's okay to be happy while still on a journey. You aren't ruining anything or jinxing your success. You are watering a plant that is you and giving yourself the nutrients needed to continue. Because in times of stress, those moments are what keep you focused and dedicated.

"Owning our story and loving ourselves through that process is the bravest thing that we'll ever do."
—Brené Brown

• • •

"To love oneself is the beginning of a life-long romance."
—Oscar Wilde

• • •

"This is not the moment to wilt into the underbrush of your insecurities. You've earned the right to grow. You're going to have to carry the water yourself."
—Cheryl Strayed

• • •

"You find peace not by rearranging the circumstances of your life,
but by realizing who you are at the deepest level."
—ECKHART TOLLE

• • •

"The most terrifying thing is to accept oneself completely."
—CARL GUSTAV JUNG

• • •

"Be gentle with yourself, learn to love yourself, to forgive
yourself, for only as we have the right attitude toward ourselves
can we have the right attitude toward others."
—WILFRED PETERSON

• • •

"Remember always that you not only have the right to be an
individual, you have an obligation to be one."
—ELEANOR ROOSEVELT

• • •

"What lies behind us and what lies before us are tiny matters compared to what lies within us."
—Ralph Waldo Emerson

• • •

"When you recover or discover something that nourishes your soul and brings joy, care enough about yourself to make room for it in your life."
—Jean Shinoda Bolen

• • •

"One of the greatest regrets in life is being what others would want you to be, rather than being yourself."
—Shannon L. Alder

• • •

Acknowledgments

This book would not be possible without all the people I have interacted with, both in person and online. In my moments of doubt, stress, worry, and panic, I had a community of people who understood and wholeheartedly supported me. From across the street to across the world, so many people provided me with valuable guidance and outlook. Thank you for helping me and investing in my personal and professional development. I'm forever grateful.

About the Author

Nacole Riccaboni is an acute care nurse practitioner working in Orlando, Florida. She was born and raised in Kissimmee, Florida, and has been a registered nurse in Florida for over ten years. She decided to become a nurse when she was involved in a motor vehicle collision as a young girl, and the nurse who cared for her sparked her interest in the nursing profession. She received a master of science in nursing degree from the University of South Alabama. She loves meeting and caring for the individuals within her community and enjoys what the nursing profession has provided and continues to provide her.

Those Quoted

Those Quoted